YOU ARE INVITED TO THE ROYAL WEDDING FEAST

British Library Cataloguing in Publication Data.

A catalogue record for this book is available from the British Library

ISBN 978 0 86071 846 8

A Commissioned Publication Printed by

MOORLEYS
Print, Design & Publishing
info@moorleys.co.uk · www.moorleys.co.uk

*Then the angel said to me,
"Blessed are those who are invited
to the wedding supper of the
Lamb!"
And he added, "These are the true
words of God."*
REVELATION 19:9

Jesus said:
*THE THIEF'S PURPOSE IS TO
STEAL KILL AND DESTROY.
MY PURPOSE IS TO GIVE THEM A
RICH AND SATISFTING LIFE*
(John 10:10)

LUCIFER/THE DEVIL
HATES ALL
HUMAN BEINGS

Recorded by Dr Siphiwe C. Nxumalo Ngubane

ACKNOWLEDGEMENTS

ALL glory, honour, power and adoration belongs to the Lord our God, to the His Son our Lord Jesus Christ and to the Holy Spirit our perfect counsellor, leader, teacher and comforter; for His love, fellowship and guidance throughout the life of humanity. I thank God for putting in my heart the desire to work with Him in His mission of reconciling humanity back to Himself. He has inspired and written this book for the advancement of His kingdom and to announce one of the greatest announcements that has ever been given to humanity, **"YOUR INVITATION TO THE ROYAL WEDDING FEAST"** through the death and resurrection of our Lord Jesus Christ.

I give God the glory for using His people who facilitated the completion of this book. I would like to thank God for my lovely husband Dumisani, who has been so inspirational from the beginning to the end of this project. He has provided a lot of insight, interpretation and commentary throughout the journey of this book. He has also provided me with rich and relevant resources from his library to enhance the writing of this book. Resources such as books, commentaries and insight into various bible texts.

I also thank God for the following young girls: Walinase Chisenga, Sinenkosi Kunene, Samiswa Ngubane and Phesheya Kunene. They participated in the pilot review and study of the book, for a number of weeks. These girls provided constructive criticisms which have enriched the lessons within this book. I am ever so grateful to Serena Rowland who has a wonderful gift and talent; she has put together all the illustrations in this book. All in all, I give God the glory for the prayers of many of His children who prayed and continue to pray that through this book His kingdom come, His will be done on earth as it is done in heaven, to the glory and honour of His precious, wonderful name, the name of our Lord Jesus Christ. AMEN.

WHY? WHY? WHY? WHY? WHY? WHY? WHY?
WHY? WHY? WHY? WHY? WHY? WHY? WHY?
WHY? WHY? WHY? WHY? WHY? WHY? WHY?
WHY? WHY? WHY? WHY? WHY? WHY? WHY?
WHY? WHY? WHY? WHY? WHY? WHY? WHY?
WHY? WHY? WHY? WHY? WHY? WHY? WHY?
WHY? WHY? WHY? WHY? WHY? WHY? WHY?
WHY? WHY? WHY? WHY? WHY? WHY? WHY?
WHY? WHY? WHY? WHY? WHY? WHY? WHY?
WHY? WHY? WHY? WHY? WHY? WHY? WHY?
WHY? WHY? WHY? WHY? WHY? WHY? WHY?
WHY? WHY? WHY? WHY? WHY? WHY? WHY?
WHY? WHY? WHY? WHY? WHY? WHY? WHY?
WHY? WHY? WHY? WHY? WHY? WHY? WHY?
WHY? WHY? WHY? WHY? WHY? WHY? WHY?
WHY? WHY? WHY? WHY? WHY? WHY? WHY?
WHY? WHY? WHY? WHY? WHY? WHY? WHY?
WHY? WHY? WHY? WHY? WHY? WHY? WHY?
WHY? WHY? WHY? WHY? WHY? WHY? WHY?
WHY? WHY? WHY? WHY? WHY? WHY? WHY?
WHY? WHY? WHY? WHY? WHY? WHY? WHY?
WHY? WHY? WHY? WHY? WHY? WHY? WHY?
WHY? WHY? WHY? WHY? WHY? WHY? WHY?
WHY? WHY? WHY? WHY? WHY? WHY? WHY?
WHY? WHY? WHY? WHY? WHY? WHY? WHY?
WHY? WHY? WHY? WHY? WHY? WHY? WHY?
WHY? WHY? WHY? WHY? WHY? WHY? WHY?
WHY?

WHY? WHY? WHY? WHY? WHY? WHY? WHY?
WHY? WHY? WHY? WHY? WHY? WHY? WHY?
WHY? WHY? WHY? WHY? WHY? WHY? WHY?
WHY? WHY? WHY? WHY? WHY? WHY? WHY?
WHY? WHY? WHY? WHY? WHY? WHY? WHY?
WHY? WHY? WHY? WHY? WHY? WHY? WHY?
WHY? WHY? WHY? WHY? WHY? WHY? WHY?
WHY? WHY? WHY? WHY? WHY? WHY? WHY?
WHY? WHY? WHY? WHY? WHY? WHY? WHY?
WHY? WHY? WHY? WHY? WHY? WHY? WHY?
WHY? WHY? WHY? WHY? WHY? WHY? WHY?
WHY? WHY? WHY? WHY? WHY? WHY? WHY?
WHY? WHY? WHY? WHY? WHY? WHY? WHY?
WHY? WHY? WHY? WHY? WHY? WHY? WHY?
WHY? WHY? WHY? WHY? WHY? WHY? WHY?
WHY? WHY? WHY? WHY? WHY? WHY? WHY?
WHY? WHY? WHY? WHY? WHY? WHY? WHY?
WHY? WHY? WHY? WHY? WHY? WHY? WHY?
WHY? WHY? WHY? WHY? WHY? WHY? WHY?
WHY? WHY? WHY? WHY? WHY? WHY? WHY?
WHY? WHY? WHY? WHY? WHY? WHY? WHY?
WHY? WHY? WHY? WHY? WHY? WHY? WHY?
WHY? WHY? WHY? WHY? WHY? WHY? WHY?
WHY? WHY? WHY? WHY? WHY? WHY? WHY?
WHY? WHY? WHY? WHY? WHY? WHY? WHY?
WHY? WHY? WHY? WHY? WHY? WHY? WHY?
WHY? WHY? WHY? WHY? WHY? WHY? WHY?
WHY?

Why am I here? Where do I come from? Where am I going? How long will I be here for? Who is God? What has he to do with me? Why is he interested in me? Why should I pay attention to him? Why is the thief coming to steal? To steal what? Why does he steal, it is bad to steal? Where does he come from? How does he benefit from stealing? Why does he kill and what/who does he kill? Who is he? Who is giving life? Is there a God? Is he powerful? What life is this, which God gives? Why does he have to love the world so much? If he created the world why did he send someone to die? As a way of showing his love, really? If he is alive why is there no peace here; wars, hunger, cruelty and bad things happening around the world? Why does he not stop all this evil in the world? Why did my father, mother, sister, relatives die? Why did he not heal their illnesses, after we even prayed and trusted him so much, why? Why? Why should I pay attention to God or Jesus, do they care about me? Why am I living with this illness? Life in abundance? What kind of life is this, yet I am already alive? If he gives life why do people die, both the good and the evil die? Why do I have this tension within me: I want to do good, but find myself doing evil? Why is there tension in me, to choose between good and evil? Why is there suffering, illnesses, poverty, all the bad things going on..........? Why is there no peace in this world, but why? What wedding is this all about? Whose wedding is it? Why am I invited? Where is the royal wedding taking place? I am not royal anyway, why I am I invited? Why? Why? Oh!!! Why? Why? Why? Why? Why? Why? Why? Why? Why?

YOU ARE INVITED TO THE ROYAL WEDDING FEAST

Contents

INTRODUCTION

Why This Book?

The purpose of this interactive book is to initiate and promote humanity's comprehensive examination into their being, origin, identity in Jesus Christ, one's purpose for being on earth and to choose one's eternal destination of the soul/spirit. To promote a holistic well-being by providing one's soul and spirit with the relevant nutrients essential to enhance maximum functioning. It is hoped that learners will be able to ponder on essential information of the soul and spirit and will therefore, be able to make informed decision(s) or choices about the eternal destination of their soul and spirit.

The desire to write this book was fuelled by the findings of a study done by Nxumalo-Ngubane, 2017, on the perceptions and experience of recovery of Swazi women living with schizophrenia. More than 85% confirmed that focusing on their spiritual being enhanced their recovery from mental illness. They talked about how they felt comforted and received hope, peace and joy as they engaged in their spiritual growth. The women talked about the fact that their recovery was enhanced by praying to God, reading the bible, attending fellowship with other believers, participating in church activities and being visited by church members, when unwell. They stated that their hope, joy and peace was re-kindled and the frequency of relapse was reduced.

The primary focus of this book is to enhance mental well-being by providing humanity with the food for the soul and spirit, allowing them to engross the self in nourishing the invisible being. The reader will have an opportunity to interact with God's word and actually realise what He says about the holistic being of humanity. By being interactive it means that the book can be read by individuals and or can be read as a group, where individuals come together (physically or virtually: zoom, skype, WhatsApp meetings, to name a few) to discuss various sections. The reader will note that some of the information is emphasised through repetition. This is important because it encourages the reader to reflect and mull over different facts, so that in the end the reader can make well informed decisions. The aim is to promote a healthy holistic human being.

The bible is the only reliable source to answer questions of humanity, including those of the spirit; it is also a rich source for the food to the soul and spirit.

Important to note is the fact that humanity is an eternal being, born with the power of the will: to make choices and decisions regarding everything, including their choice of where they want to spend their eternal life. On the other hand, humanity does not have the liberty to either choose where and when they are born, or where and when they will die. Additionally, while they can choose where they want to spend their eternal life, they have no control over the consequences of their choices. The illustration below aims to further clarify the above paragraph.

Below is a table with two columns: first, some of the things that humanity has no control over and the second has a list of some of the things to which humanity has the ability to control through the power of their will. Please add other items which you believe fit on either columns.

HUMANITY: BODY, SOUL, SPIRIT	
Uncontrollable	**Humanity's Choice/Will**
Birth, date, time, location	Friends
Death (excl. suicide) date, time, location	Where to live
Parents	How you treat others
Skin colour	Values and beliefs
Consequences for the choice of eternal destination	Eternal destination
Inner vacuum to worship God	Who fills the vacuum

The purpose of this book is to share information about the two destinations of humanity, so that they can make informed choices. It is essential to make informed choices, it helps avoid regrets at a later time. Lack of knowledge is dangerous because it can lead to death, as stated in Hosea 4:6: *"My people are destroyed because of lack of knowledge......"* As such, this book is not about a particular religion, it is all about the reality of humanity, their origin, components and eternity.

This book is not meant to exalt the enemy, nor is it a vehicle to blame humanity for things happening around their lives. Also, this book is not intended to scare humanity about eternal destruction, but it is meant to reveal the heart of our heavenly Father's abundant love for His asset. This book intends to explore God's greatest plan of salvation: restoring humanity back to Himself. Perhaps helping humanity to better understand their origin, identity and eternal destination.

Perhaps we can think about the different types of cars available in the market. If one chooses to purchase a Mercedes-Benz, when the car requires replacement of parts it is sensible for them to go back to the Mercedes-Benz manufacturer to get a replace. Using a similar car part from a Toyota or hundi manufacturer or counterfeit parts does not only guarantee the car of its poor function and performance, but it is also a gate way to its untimely death. Likewise, only God and NONE OTHER is the giver of life (through His spirit Genesis 2:7) to all humanity. As the source and manufacturer of human spirit, He qualifies to feed and nurture this aspect of humanity. This means then that other sources trying to feed and nurture the spirit of humanity are counterfeits, so that using these hinders the maximum function and performance of the human being.

It is possible that a lot of us have unanswered questions, perhaps regarding personally experienced events, life in general or pertaining to why, who, what, and where a human being originated and or ends when they move out of this world. It is hoped that the opportunity to reflect, think and rethink over certain passages and situations will stimulate further research and understanding of God's plans and desires for humanity.

This Title

The events occurring at the two eternal locations are very unique and different. These will be discussed in detail within this book. The title of this book comes from one event which will take place in heaven. Jesus came to this world (as a groom) in order to redeem humanity from the snares of Lucifer, the devil. Those who accept Jesus' love are sometimes referred to as His bride. On his departure to heaven Jesus promised that he was going to prepare mansions for his bride. The celebration of the welcoming of Jesus' bride is one of the biggest events which will take place in heaven. In short, Jesus died on the cross so that humanity will not die, but have eternal life (John 3:16). Following his victory over sin, Jesus is inviting humanity to His wedding feast in heaven, where his bride (those who choose to accept his love) will be welcomed to heaven during a wedding ceremony; there will be endless fellowship and communion with God the Father; Son and the Holy Spirit. So, today Jesus is calling: ***"YOU ARE INVITED TO THE ROYAL WEDDING FEAST."***

Exercise

Please imagine that you have an appointment to have a chat with God tomorrow, at 09:00 am and the only thing you have to do is ask him questions. Write down as many questions as you can in preparation for this meeting.

From the above exercise it is clear that we are beings with many questions. Maybe this is why humanity engage in so much research; to seek facts and evidence for various phenomena, about the past, present and future. This has and is possibly bringing about a number of theories regarding certain events and experiences, for example *the big bang theory.*

While all these theories and explanations are clearly delineated, it is significant to highlight that the core root and foundation of discussions within this book is the Bible. The question is WHY the Bible instead of other scientific books? Who wrote the Bible? Why does it have authority over things and over humanity?

What the Bible Says About Itself

We can refer back to the Bible to get many answers to many questions. As you go through the lessons in this book, the Holy Spirit will help answer a lot of questions, including but not limited to the ones listed above. Before looking further into the Bible's uniqueness, the quotations below provide an insight into various contemporary perspectives of the Bible.

"Within the covers of the Bible are the answers for all the problems men face." Ronald Reagan.

"I believe the Bible is the best gift God has ever given to man. All the good from the saviour of the world is communicated to us through this book." Abraham Lincoln.

"The Bible was not given for our information, but for our transformation." Dwight Lyman Moody.

"A Bible that's falling apart usually belongs to someone who isn't." Charles H. Surgeon.

An opponent of the Bible stated:

"You can point to the alleged miracles of the Bible or any other religious text, but they are nothing but old stories fabricated by man and then exaggerated over the time." Dan Brown.

It is Unique

The Bible has outstanding attributes that makes it distinct from all other books. Please identify and analyse the attributes within the following texts:

2 Timothy 3:16-17

Jeremiah 23:29

John 10:35

Hebrews 4:12

2 Corinthians 5:17

Matthew 28:19-20

Isaiah 40:8; Mark 13:31

Psalms 119:105

Psalms 119:130

John 1:1

Isaiah 55:1

Ezekiel 3:3; Proverbs 16:24

John 4: 24; 15:3

Psalms 107:20

In conclusion, the Bible is God's word, written by human beings who were inspired by God. We believe and trust in the God who created heaven and earth. Through faith we believe in the one and only living God. God is the only creator of the universe and all that is in it. This means that God is in charge and in control of everything. By faith we believe that the only one and true God created heaven and earth and all that is in it (Hebrews 11:2). The Bible is the Word of God. In John 1:1 we learn that the Word is Jesus. God used the Word to create the world and this Word (Jesus) was in existence even before the world was created (John 1:1-5). As we continue with our study, we shall explore how God's control over everything is related to man's will and choices.

Prologue

One of the phrases which describe God is *'The Ancient of Days'* (Isaiah 43:13; Daniel 7:9), he has been in existence way back, even before the beginning of time. He is all powerful and loving, the *'Great I am'*, in charge and in control of everything in heaven and earth. God is worshipped by multitudes of angelic beings in heaven. A long time ago, before he created heaven and earth, the angel in charge of worship was Lucifer, the greatest worshipper and light bearer.

Unfortunately, a disruption occurred in heaven, Lucifer became envious of God, he was jealous and proud; and wanted to be worshipped like God (Ezekiel 28:17). God will never share his glory with anyone (Isaiah 42:8); Lucifer then became God's adversary (Satan). He was taken out of heaven and was thrown into the earth (Ezekiel 28:17). God has prepared the lake of fire where Lucifer will be endlessly tortured and tormented, because of this pride and arrogance (Revelation 20:10).

During his rebellion from God Lucifer was followed by one third of God's angels (Revelation 12:4). The fallen angels work with Lucifer, to fight God, every day, until their eternal placement in hell. In His innovation, God then created heaven and earth, it took him five days. He then created a human being in his image. Adam was the first human being. God used the dust of the earth to create humanity's physical body, but man was helpless, until God breathed his breath into his nostrils. Adam then became a living being.

God then took one of Adam's ribs and put it into the second human being: Eve, Adam's wife. God blessed them, assigned them to be fruitful and multiply, be in charge of all creation and to overcome the world. God loves humanity, they are his treasure and they have his spirit which makes them alive. After creating Adam and Eve God would come from heaven to have fellowship with them, spending quality time with them in the Garden of Eden; what a glorious fellowship they had! God's love for humanity is also revealed by the fact that he gave them the power of *their will;* to make their own choices without any pressure. God showed them around the garden, informing them that they could eat of any tree in the garden, except one tree at the centre of the garden.

Ever since creation God's adversary, Satan uses all tricks and tactics to influence humanity to choose him and duplicate his rebellion against God's plan and will. Satan influenced Eve to eat the forbidden fruit and she also gave it to her husband, he ate it. They sinned against God and as a result, their relationship with God was seriously disturbed. One of the consequences of falling into sin was that human beings will die; their bodies return to the dust from which they were taken and their souls go the lake of fire, a place originally prepared for Satan.

Nevertheless, because of his immeasurable love and mercy, God made a plan of reconciliation with humanity; to restore the broken relationship with his treasure. He sent his only son, the Lord Jesus Christ to die in their place. Again, God is such a gentleman, he does not use any force or pressure. Anyone who accepts Jesus as their Lord and personal saviour will not die, but will enjoy eternal life; an everlasting restored relationship and fellowship with God. Although humanity's physical body dies and they are buried to the ground, their spirit does not. The spirit of those who have accepted Jesus as their Lord and Saviour awaits the big day of the wedding feast. Yet, the spirit of those who do not accept Jesus Christ as their personal saviour awaits eternal destruction in the lake of fire. Again, the power of choice is fundamental, those who will attend the wedding feast can only make the choice while they are alive, in this world. **HUMANITY IS INVITED TO THE ROYAL WEDDING FEAST. ATTENDANCE IS BY CHOICE: ACCEPTING JESUS CHRIST AS LORD AND SAVIOUR, INTO ONE'S HEART.**

Please make notes below on your thoughts about the following:

The Word of God.

What makes Christianity different?

A Glimpse of Heaven

LESSON 1
Before Genesis 1:1

The aim of this chapter is to provide an understanding of the origins and intentions of the enemy for humanity. It is hoped that this understanding will enhance humanity's ability to make informed decisions as they peruse activities of daily living, in all areas of their being: body, soul and spirit.

Before the earth was created, we see heaven and the angels-worshipping the awesome, most high God, not out of duty, but in awe of his glory. The angels marvel at his beauty and glory, then prostrate at his feet while proclaiming *"Holy, holy, holy is the Lord God all mighty."* Nehemiah 9:6; Revelations 4:6-11; 7:11-12. Opposite is a picture to illustrate the throne of God.

The Origin and Fall of Lucifer

Please read the following texts: Ezekiel 28:13-17; Isaiah 14:12-15; Revelation 12:7-12, then make notes below.

In regard to understanding who Lucifer is, what insight do you have from the above text, regarding the following:

Who is Lucifer?

What is the meaning of Lucifer?

Where does he come from?

What led to his relocation?

Where does he live today?

As we have realised from the above readings Lucifer was a leader of worship in heaven and had a very important role and gift (Ezekiel 28:14). His role is clearly revealed in the meaning of his name a 'shining one, light bearer or morning star.' Lucifer was the greatest or the leader of all the angels.

Unfortunately, Lucifer stated competing with God. He became very proud and wanted to be worshipped like God. Because God will never share His glory with anyone (Isaiah 42:8) Lucifer was removed from his position as the leader of worship and from heaven. He was cast to earth (Revelation 12:9). Lucifer rebelled with other angels, he uses them today to constantly fight against God's asset, humanity. He then acquired different names which are associated with his roles. He is called: the devil which means 'accuser' of those who choose Jesus Christ. 'Satan' means an adversary, because he is God's enemy; he is also known as a tempter, the murder, a liar, a serpent, dragon. Further deliberation on these names and his roles will be discussed later on in the book. Let us reflect on some of Lucifer's goals and motives as written in the bible. Regarding the attributes of Lucifer, refer to the Bible references listed in the table below. Please give examples of how Lucifer's attributes are manifested in real life.

Lucifer's Attributes	Bible Source	Real Life Examples
A thief, a killer, destroyer	John 10:10; 1 Peter 5:8	
A liar, a father of lies	John 8:44	
Clever and Deceptive	2 Corinthians 11:14	
Pretender	2 Corinthians 11:14	

2

A tempter	Matthew 4:3; 1 Thessalonians 3:5	
Evil reproducer	Matthew 13:38,39; 1 John 5:19	
A ruler of the kingdom of the air	Ephesians 2:2	
Blinds people	2 Corinthians 4:4	
Ancient dragon, leads people stray	Revelations 12:9	
An accuser of brethren	Revelation 12:10	
Roams the earth	Job 1:7; 2:2	
Harms and kills as God permits	Job 1:12; 2:6	
Awaits destruction	Ezekiel 28:19; Revelation 20:2,3,10	
Runs when resisted	James 4:7	

It is very importance to always remember that Lucifer lived in heaven and knows all about God the Father, the Son and the Holy Spirit. He is fully aware of this beautiful, peaceful and holy place (Isaiah 14:12). Unfortunately, he can never be allowed in heaven anymore, but has a place prepared for him and all his followers, in eternal destruction – hell (Matthew 25:41). Consequently, Satan is very angry about this and he realises that he does not have much time (Revelations 12:12). His motive is to make sure that no humanity enters heaven, but that rather, they join him in his place of continuous torture and torment (Matthew 25:41-46). The question is why does he target humanity, what is so special about human beings which makes Satan to pursue.

Please have a quiet time and think about the information above. What does the above information mean to you? Think about how you should relate to Satan.

In the subsequent lessons we will deliberate on God's asset and how Lucifer attempts to accomplish his mission, by influencing humanity to be his host for causing and doing evil all around God's earth. For now, we will look at how God meticulously created the world we live in.

LESSON 2
God's Spectacular Ingenuity

The main focus of this chapter is to reflect and ponder on the authority of God as the source, founder and creator of everything on earth (Psalms 102:25) and to realise how God then allowed humanity to share and participate in his role of taking care of his creation; the assignment to be a steward of all his creation and have dominion over everything (Genesis 2:15; 1:28).

His Mighty Power and Authority

God's power and authority is manifest in his ability to create this dynamic world; in a very 'short' period of time. His creation also reveals God's mighty power to speak and make the world to come to being; no wonder theologians refer to Him as **Omnipotent**; *'Omni'* means all and *'potent'* stands for powerful. God is in charge of heaven and earth; he is in control. This was affirmed by the Westminster Confession of Faith written in the seventeenth century, stating: *'God the great creator of all things doth uphold, direct, dispose and govern all creatures, actions and things from the greatest even to the least, by his most wise and holy providence,'* (The Word for Today by Bob Gass, October, page 59, Autumn 2019 August/September/October).

God created this world by speaking, using the Word. The Word existed before the beginning, He was with God, before creation (John 1:1-3). This is Jesus the son of the living God, also referred to as the Word. God created everything through His Word. His Word is very powerful, indicating His unique authority which no other being possesses, but God alone. God spoke and things came to be; his Word has authority (Psalms 33:9). Hence, He is also referred to as **Omniscient**, because He is *'Omni'* all; *'scient'* which stands for 'knowing.' God knows everything, even the amount of hair on one's head (Psalms 139:1-4; Matthew 10:29-30). God is the only one who is present at all places at the same time, even the devil does not have this mighty attribute. He is **Omnipresent**. As already realised above, Omni stands for all, meaning that God is present all around the heaven and earth at the same time. David stated this in Psalms 139:7-10.

The Word (Jesus) later became flesh, as stated in John 1:14. The question would be why did the Word/ Jesus bother to become flesh and why is this so significant? To restore God's image which was lost in the Garden of Eden when humanity fell into sin, restoring creation back to its initial state (Luke 19:10). It took God five days to create heaven and earth, He then created man on the sixth day and then rested on the seventh day. Initially, the earth was shapeless and empty, there was darkness in the deep, yet the Spirit of the God was hovering around (Genesis 1:2). During creation God spoke and two main activities occurred: there was the **formation** of heaven and earth and then God **filled** all which he had formed with appropriate forms of life. God formed heavens, landmasses and the waters; he then filled all three areas with relevant forms of live.

On the *first day* God created light, and he separated it from darkness; He called the light day and the darkness He named night (Genesis 1:3-5). God then separated water into two parts those above the firmament (atmosphere) and those below the firmament (Genesis 1:6-8). This means that on the *second day* God created the waters which are wrapped up in the clouds and the waters which cover the seas. From the beginning of creation God clearly demonstrated the importance of separation. Please list some of the things which God separated during creation.

Further deliberation of separation is discussed later in the subsequent lessons.

God made and separated the dry ground and the sea on the *third day.* He then filled the earth with plants and decreed that each would reproduce (Genesis 1:9-10; 11-13). On the *fourth day* God filled the firmament with heavenly bodies: the sun, moon and stars, planets

(Genesis 1:14-19). He then allocated duties to each of these bodies, to mark days, months, years and seasons.

On the *fifth day* God filled the sky and the waters with creatures: birds that fly and sea animals (Genesis 1:20-23). God did not just declare that what he had done was good, but he also blessed the creatures giving them the ability to reproduce.

On the *sixth day* God first commanded that the earth must produce all sort of animals and he also gave them the ability to reproduce and multiply (Genesis 1:24-25). There seems to be a significant transition after the creation of animals. God moved onto his next creation. While God spoke when creating all the above, he paused and discussed with the trinity regarding the creation of humanity.

Please take some time and read Genesis 1:26. Make a note of your thoughts and insight on this verse in relation to:

The meeting about creating humanity.

The purpose of humanity's existence.

Throughout his creation, God affirmed that what He had created was good and beautiful. This confirms the deep-rooted goodness of God and his creation. The goodness of creation displays God's splendour and beauty, so that nature, every creature and creation declares the goodness of God. Therefore, humanity has no excuse to say that there is no God (Roman 1:20). In other words, as humanity sees God's creation they are amazed by His innovation and His spectacular ingenuity (Psalms 19:1).

What are your thoughts, feelings and ideas about God's authority?

After all His creativity God rested on the *seventh day,* the Sabbath. God blessed the seventh day and made it holy, because he rested from all the world's creation. The next chapter examines God's detailed creation of humanity. This will hopefully enhance a vivid insight into humanity's origin, role, identity and destination as stipulated by God their creator.

LESSON 3
God's Asset: Humanity

The focus of this chapter is on the deliberation of how God created human beings, their distinct components and characteristics. Two of the components of humanity are discussed within this lesson and the third will be dealt with in lesson 4.

You Are God's Asset

Just before His rest on the seventh day, God created man and woman (Adam and Eve) "in His own image" Genesis 1:26. Humanity is a true reflection of God, man is like God. He then breathed His spirit in Adam's nostrils and he became a living being. This means that humans have attributes that are similar to those of God. They are distinct, peculiar, fearful and wonderfully made beings (Psalms 139:14). Humanity is at the apex of God's heart; they are his treasure and are superior to all other creations. God loves humanity, because they are his special creation, made with his hands and are a living being because of his spirit he breathed through their nostrils.

Similar to God: humanity is three in one. There is God the Father, Son and the Holy Spirit. Humanity is also divided into three parts: body, soul and spirit. This is clearly stated by Paul in 1 Thessalonians 5:23. Aristotle stated that humans are *"more than the sum of their total."* Implying that humans are not just made up of the visible physical body. A human being is made up of physical material (dust) the body which we can see and touch, he is also made up of invisible materials; not seen with the naked eyes: the soul, spirit, intellect, the will, emotion and the conscience. The physical body is temporal and soon returns back to the earth from which it came (Genesis 3:19). The invisible aspects exist beyond the physical lifespan, they are eternal (Ecclesiastes 12:7).

The immortal aspects, however, (spirit, soul) make up the whole personality of a human being. These two words: spirit and soul will be used interchangeable throughout this book. The bible states that the soul and the spirit are the primary immaterial aspect of humanity, the human body is the physical container that holds the invisible human while they live in this world (2 Corinthians 5:1). It is of great significance to note that the physical body is visible and temporal, but the spiritual aspect is not only invisible, it exits forever (2 Corinthians 4:18).

The spirit, even though not visible, is very important and lasts forever. It is God's treasure, a free gift that makes humanity alive. Please read and mull over the verse in 2 Corinthians 4:18, then make notes on your understanding and feelings about the eternity of the invisible you.

All three aspects of humanity are essential for the whole being to be complete. Each of these aspects of humanity have their unique needs. Please take some time to make a list of some of the needs, for each of the aspects of humanity. Thinks about things which makes each area thrive and maintain optimal function.

Body

Soul

Spirit

Following the process of responding to the recent question, how did you find retrieving the needs of each aspect? For example, the number of items in each area, how easy was it to retrieve the needs of each area? Which area was the easiest/most challenging to retrieve?

Personally, when I did this exercise, I realised that the needs of the body are easy to retrieve and I had less struggle brainstorming them. However, the needs of the soul and the spirit were difficult to identify. As a result, I found that my list for the body's needs was longer than the other two. Perhaps you also had the same experience: YES/NO. If yes, what do you think is the reason?

Later on, in this chapter we will deliberate on the above. For now, we will continue to explore humanity's God given assignments. After creating Adam and Eve God put them in the Garden of Eden, then He gave them assignments and left them to live as they desired. Every evening God spent quality time with Adam and Eve, there was fellowship and communion and they were very close to God (Genesis

3:8). This relationship was disrupted, as we are going to explore further on in the book. It is so humbling to realise God's unconditional love for humanity, that he would leave his beautiful place in heaven to spend time to fellowship and commune with humanity. God loves humanity. He even made humanity to be in charge of His creation. Please take some time to explore the assignments given to humanity according to Genesis 1:26 & 28, also state what these assignments are and what they mean to you.

As already discussed in the previous paragraph humanity was given authority to rule over all creation, to be fruitful and multiply and to overcome, subdue and have dominion over all creation. After creating humanity God then took them to the Garden of Eden and gave them responsibilities (Genesis 2:15). God made humanity the steward of nature; he assigned man to till the soil. It is interesting to note that this was initially God's role, but because of his immeasurable love for humanity and the fact that man is made in his image, God is sharing His massive responsibility with humanity, his asset.

The dust from which man was created had no life, Adam (the first man) laid on the floor lifeless, he did not move nor was he able to function, until God put his spirit (breath) in him through his nostrils; Adam then became a living being (Genesis 2:7). Without God's invisible spirit humanity is non-functional, he is mere dust. God gives all human beings His spirit, they are only functional and have life because of God's breath. All living humans have God's spirit (Numbers 16:22), and as such God has the ability to take it back to himself at any time he chooses to. What insight do you get from the above paragraph, and the verse in Numbers 16:22. As you reflect on this section please focus on the section where Moses acknowledged that God is the sole provider of the spirit, within Numbers 16:22.

The Visible Being

According to Genesis 2:7 humanity was created from the dust/mud; God took the dust of the earth and crafted humanity and this is composed of the physical body which we see with our naked eyes. The name 'Adam' means "taken out of the ground" (The Wiersbe Bible Commentary, page 16). God then brought the body to life by giving it his breath, via his nostrils and man became a **living** soul/being (Genesis 2:7). This means that not only has God created humanity's physical body, he also gave them life, without God's spirit humanity does not exist, it would just be mud.

As an innovative God, He decided to paint the mud into different colours. One image of God with different colours. Perhaps, as an innovative God, He wanted to break the monotony of having one colour in His world. God saw it beautiful to have variety in skin the colours of humanity. Interestingly, the colour of blood for humanity is red and they all use the same air - oxygen (God's spirit) to sustain life. *"And He has made from one blood every nation of men to dwell on all the face of the earth......"* Acts 17:26.

Please take some time to make notes on your thoughts and feelings about the differences of humanity, considering the following: colours, location, culture, to name a few.

Below is an illustration of some of God's variation when colouring the mud.

Diversity of the Mud

Nourishing the Mud

The physical body gets nourished with vitamins and minerals from the food we eat daily; its optimum function is enhanced by keeping physically fit through exercise, rest and sleep. The body's needs are satisfied by physical things - these are all visible and tangible. If deprived from any of the needs, the body becomes diseased. Please brainstorm on some of the diseases which may develop in the body as a result of a lack of the essential elements which enhance the body's optimum function.

Humans are alive; able to move their physical being (mud) because of the spirit they were given by God. There are times when the physical person becomes unwell needing support with air from the external environment, in order to sustain life. The advancement of technology has made this possible, where oxygen is given to the physical body when it fails to automatically take in oxygen from the air. Oxygen can be administered in various ways, such as artificial ventilation or through nostrils (see the picture to illustrate this). However, the sovereign authority of God is evident when humanity's endeavourers to sustain life fails. This is when God takes away his spirit from the physical body (mud) and the person is declared dead.

While the present body can be destroyed or damaged by various situations, nobody can destroy humanity's soul and spirit (Matthew 10:28). Instead, God has promised to give humanity a new immortal body, which will never be affected by illness, diseases or any form of destruction (Philippines 3:21). The question is: what happens to the soul? Where does God take his soul? A further deliberation on this subject follows in subsequent lessons. What constitutes the other aspects of the human being, the invisible being?

The Asset of God in the Mud

The Invisible Being

As already highlighted human beings are not just mere visible bodies, they are also spiritual beings, that is, they are made up of the invisible: **soul and spirit.** Both are mysteriously linked or connected to each other to form what the Bible sometimes refers to as the 'heart' (Psalms 51:10, 12). These two invisible aspects live in and influence the physical being (Proverbs 4:23; 2 Corinthians 5:1): **SPIRIT + SOUL = HEART.** The heart is central to emotions and the will. It is important to pay very close attention to the invisible being: soul and spirit, especially because, being invisible it is easy to neglect these aspects, perhaps not deliberately, but maybe because of a lack of knowledge and understanding of how God created his asset, YOU.

Humanity is not only referred to as living beings, they are also known as living souls (Genesis 2:7 NIV; KVJ). Within their spirit humanity has an empty space/vacuum which can never be filled or satisfied by anyone/thing, other than the presence of God in their lives. Solomon, the wisest and richest person who has ever lived in this world did research in an attempt to satisfy or fill this vacuum. He concluded: *"Everything is wearisome beyond description. No matter how much we see, we are never satisfied. No matter how much we hear, we are not content."* **Ecclesiastes 1:8.**

"......Everything is meaningless—like chasing the wind." **Ecclesiastes 2:17.**

Solomon's conclusion was: *"......Here now is my final conclusion: Fear God and obey his commands, for this is everyone's duty. God will judge us for everything we do, including every secret thing, whether good or bad."* **Ecclesiastes 12:13, 14.**

The **soul** consists of a number of aspects: the senses, the mind (where we have the conscience), the will and the emotions. These aspects of the soul are pivotal in humanity's interaction and contact with each other. The soul lives within the physical body and therefore, the two are well connected. While God created a clear and pure human soul, the human soul was contaminated by the entrance of sin when they ate the forbidden fruit in the Garden of Eden. As a result, the soul is primarily attuned to the things of the world/earth, such that the changes

16

in an individual's mood and feelings is influenced by things happening around them. Most things around the earth are unsteady and changeable. Consequently, humans who allow their soul to control their lives are never at rest. For example, they might be overly concerned about what other people think and say about them. Paul has a solution to this challenge, according to Romans 12:2. To refuse to conform to the things of the world but allow the Holy Spirit to re-educate and re-direct one's mind. This can only be accomplished by using the will of humanity: choosing to let the Holy Spirit be in control. Our heart is central to our emotional will. The will allows us to make decisions (Joshua 24:15).

The Will

God then gave Adam and Eve instructions: that they could eat from all the fruits in the garden, but not the tree planted at the centre of the garden (Genesis 2:17). While Adam was away Satan approached Eve in a form of a snake (Genesis 3:1), pretending to verify God's instructions. He argued with Eve that the fruit was okay to eat; that God did not tell them the truth, because he did not want them to know the difference between right and wrong (Genesis 3: 4, 5).

How do you think Eve could have best responded to Satan's proposal in order to avoid the trap of falling into sin? As you respond to this question you could think about:

Spending time in solitude

Critical thinking in decision making

Association

Consultation before making a conclusion

Take some time to think about the above situation, imagine you are Eve.

What would you have done?

How would you have reacted to the snake's proposal?

It is important to note that the devil also gave humanity information, but his was contrary to the instructions given by God. Even though the devil did not force Eve to eat the fruit, his approach pressured Eve to disobey God's instructions. He claimed that God had given humanity wrong information, arguing that they were not going to die, but their eyes would be opened so that they would *be like God* (Genesis 3:5). The devil used a similar concept which led to his fall: he wanted to *be like God*. He lied and deceived Eve and he still deceives humanity today. Lucifer also targeted Eve's will, so that she had the choice to either accept his deceptive information or stick to God's instructions. Unfortunately, Eve looked at the tree and saw that the fruit was good, she ate and gave some to her husband to eat. Adam and Eve fell into temptation from Lucifer. They fell into sin.

In his quest to destroy humanity's relationship with God, Lucifer uses a number of tactics. Please read the text in Genesis 3:1-5. How do you think Lucifer wants humanity to perceive God and His Word?

It is important to note that up to this day Lucifer continues to use the same strategies as highlighted, his motive is to steal humanity from their source of origin and kill the communion and fellowship between God and humanity so that humanity will join him in the eternal destruction in hell.

God gave humanity the independence to choose, according to his (man's) *will.* God did not directly tell Adam and Eve that Lucifer was on the earth where he placed them, he only informed them that if they disobeyed his command they would surely die (Genesis 2:17). However, God informed them about two things which shows that there is evil in the world. That there was a *tree of the knowledge of good and evil*; and that their assignment was to *subdue the world* (Genesis 1:28). Since creation God does not impose anything on humanity, but why? This is because of His immeasurable love, God loves humanity and He desires them to be autonomous: humanity has been designed in His image. God gives humanity information and the liberty to choose what they desire. Every human being has the power of their **WILL**.

In other words, even though God is in charge of everything, including the will of humans, He (God) allows them to make their own choices. Dr R.C. Sproul stated it very clearly: *'God's sovereign providence stands over and above our action. He works out his will through the actions of human will, without violating the freedom of those human will,'* (The Word for Today by Bob Gass, October, 2019). This means that even though God is sovereign and is in control of everything including men's will, He is still loving and allows humans the liberty to make their own choices. Meanwhile, God has also informed humanity about the consequences of the choices they make (Genesis 2:17; Deuteronomy 30:15-20; John 3:16).

In the book of Genesis it is clear that both humanity and the snake incurred the consequences for breaking God's commands and these continue to affect humans and the snake today (Genesis 3: 11-19). Please identify the consequences for each of the parties which were involved in breaking God's command and reflect on how each makes you feel:

Snake

My feelings

Woman

My feelings

Man

My feelings

Please refer to the first lesson of this book (Lucifer's Attributes) and read Genesis 3:1-6. Enumerate how Lucifer actually used his attributes to tempt Adam and Eve:

Lucifer's Attributes	How He Used Them to Tempt Adam and Eve
Crafty	Influencing Eve to question God's word/instructions.
Liar	Telling Eve that she will not die from eating the fruit. Twisting truth: letting Eve know she will gain morality from the tree.

Prideful	Telling Eve she will become like God when she eats from the tree.

Do you think that the fall of humanity into sin could have been avoided? YES/NO. Please elaborate on the reasons for whichever response you picked and state how you endeavour to prevent falling into sin when you are tempted.

It is interesting to note that the serpent was the most cunning of all the animals in the garden and so the devil used it to lead humanity astray. Up to this day Lucifer influences humanity to choose his will versus that of God. As a result, there is a constant tension in humanity; the fight between right and wrong; choosing God or Lucifer. A further discussion on this subject follows in lesson 5.

Below is a visual summary of the three interrelated components of humanity and a summary of some of the characteristics of each. You can place your picture on the left side of the page, where there is a blank circle. The aim of this diagram is to succinctly show that *you are more than the sum of your total'* as stated by Aristotle. God created you with three essential and integrated components, they individually have unique needs which when unmet leads to disequilibrium of the whole, YOU.

The Trio of Humanity

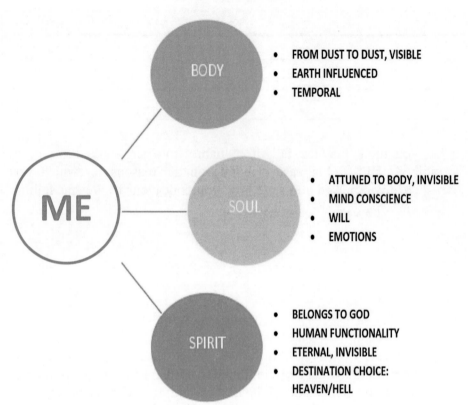

For a further visualisation of the relationship between the soul, body and the spirit please see the sketch overleaf, a contribution from W. Chisenga, one of the participants who piloted the study of these lessons.

Body + Soul + Spirit = Humanity

Before deliberating on the third aspect of humanity; the 'spirit', please make a note of a few keywords that stand out to you from the two aspects of humanity already discussed. Also indicate why these are of significance to you.

Body

Significance of the above

Soul

Significance of the above

LESSON 4
God's Asset in the Mud: His Spirit

The aim of this chapter is to deliberate on the core aspect of humanity, which makes them 'beings,' without which humanity does not exist: God's spirit. God breathed his breath into Adam's nostrils and he became a living being (Genesis 2:7). Further exploration is made on the things which nourish the spirit and how these compare to those of the soul and body.

The Real You: God's Spirit

After he was created from the ground Adam was useless, he laid helpless on the ground. Then God put His spirit through Adam's nostrils, Adam then became a living being. Therefore: humanity is *the mud + God's spirit = life.* From the previous paragraphs we realise that the death of humanity is one of the consequences of falling into sin (Genesis 3:19). As it is today the physical body dies when God takes away His spirit and the mud returns to the earth from which it came. The spirit does not die, it remains assigned to whom it was initially given. Adam and Eve fell into sin and they realised that they were naked. God then devised an initial temporal plan to cover up man's nakedness. He killed an animal and used the animal's skin to clothe Adam and Eve (Genesis 3:21).

The fall of humanity into sin separated them from having a smooth harmonious relationship and fellowship with God. Sin distances/separates humanity from God (Isaiah 59:2). He is a holy God and will not stay where sin abides. This separation marked the beginning of **Satan's evil spiritual lineage** in the life of humanity. After falling into sin humanity was destined for eternal death in hell. We have already seen in lesson 3 that humanity is God's image, his asset; He put His spirit in humanity and desires to commune with them. Because of His love for humanity God then brought a permanent solution to restore the initial plan of fellowship and communion, which was interrupted by Lucifer in the Garden of Eden. God gave His only son, Jesus, to come to the world and save humanity from sin, by dying on the cross of calvary (John 3:16).

Please read and reread the previous verse (John 3:16) and make notes below about what it means to you.

The death and resurrection of Jesus brings about the restoration of humanity's spiritual lineage, providing them with an opportunity to be born again and receive eternal life. Perhaps you have noted that there are two spiritual destinations offered by God within the verse above: life and death. Those who choose to believe in the son of God (Jesus Christ) receive a changed spiritual lineage. The genetic formation of sin is removed and replaced by God's genes of righteousness; they are born again and become children of God. They have ETERNAL LIFE. On the contrary, those who choose to reject Jesus remain within the devil's lineage, their spiritual genetic formation has sin within and they are destined for ETERNAL DESTRUCTION.

There are two types of death; physical death and spiritual death. When the time comes for a human being's end of the physical life, God takes His spirit and places it at a destination chosen by the owner. The physical body is returned (burial or cremation) to the earth from which it was made. While this marks the end of the physical body, the spiritual person does not die, but lives forever (eternally). This confirms that (concerning humanity) the visible things are temporal and those things which are unseen are permanent (2 Corinthians 4:18). The spirit's destination is determined by that particular individual when both are still together (body and spirit) on this earth; when the person is still alive. Rejecting Jesus Christ while still alive on earth is a declaration that one chooses to go to hell where there is eternal destruction. On the other hand, accepting Jesus Christ as one's personal Lord and Saviour leads to eternal life John 3:16.

Humanity's spirit belongs to God, it is a gift from Him. God is in full control of the humanity's spirit. However, He holds the owner accountable for the choices one makes regarding their eternal destination. There are two destinations of the spirit from which humans have to choose: heaven or hell.

This has come about as the result of the fall of Lucifer, as already discussed at the beginning of this book. It is very important to note that, because of the fall of Lucifer God did not only remove Lucifer from heaven, God has also prepared hell for his eternal torture and torment. Hell was created for Lucifer; this is where he will face his eternal destruction (Matthew 25:41-46; Revelation 14:11). HELL WAS NEVER MADE FOR HUMANITY.

Take some time to reflect on the two destinations of the spirit. What are your thoughts and feelings about each one?

Hell

Heaven

It is important to note that when he fell into sin, Lucifer left heaven with a third of God's angels (Jude 1:6). As we have already seen, he was a great worshipper of God, he knows the beauty of heaven and a lot of what humanity have not seen regarding God and heaven. Satan's mission is to get as many people as he can to follow him into the eternal destruction. His goal is to influence God's human beings to denounce God so that they no longer have a relationship with their creator and this is the doorway to eternal separation from God, which ends up in hell (John 10:10).

What are your thoughts and feelings about Lucifer and his mission?

All in all, humans do not die (Ecclesiastics 3:11; John 11: 25 & 26; Hebrew 2:14). God's sole purpose for creating humans is to have an endless relationship and fellowship with them (Genesis 3:8; Isaiah 43:7; 1 Corinthians 1:9). As such, all human beings do not die, it is the physical being (body) which dies, all because Adam and Eve listened to the devil and ate the forbidden fruit (Genesis 3:19; Romans 5: 12).

God then showed His love by sending His only son, the Lord Jesus Christ, to die once and for all (John 3:16) so that even though our physical bodies dies, our spirit being will be with Him forever, only by accepting Jesus Christ into our hearts and making him to be in charge of our lives, while we live on earth (Romans 5:19). Besides living with Jesus in heaven when the physical body dies, those who accept Jesus as their Lord and Saviour have their names written in The Book of Life or The Lamb's Book of Life (Luke 10:20). This is very important because God will gather humanity one day and will read the names written in The Book of Life (Matthew 25:31-34, 41; Revelation 3:5; Revelation 20:15). Those whose names will not be found in The Book of Life will be taken to eternal destruction (hell) where death will be taken away: there will be crying, torture, wailing and gnashing of teeth; day and night. This is the second death, the death of the soul: eternal separation from God (Matthew 13:50; Revelation 21:8). The book of life does not only contain the names of all those who accept the Lord Jesus as their personal saviour, it also has an account of their deeds while living in this world (Psalms 69:28; Revelation 3:5; 21:27).

Jesus came to this world to give humanity eternal life, for the spirit. In other words, instead of going to hell (eternal destruction) the spirit of those who choose to accept Jesus Christ as their Lord and Saviour goes to heaven. Jesus reversed the consequences of sin by dying on the cross and rising up on the third day (John 3:16; Colossians 2:11-15). God planned for the eternal salvation of humanity ahead of time: *"The seed of the woman will crush your head"* (Genesis 3:15). He sent Jesus to die at the cross, to pay the price in the place of humanity.

Humanity does not need to die, because the powers of the devil were completely taken away from him at the cross (Revelation 1:18). Satan's initial plan was to destroy Jesus by hanging him at the cross, little did he know that this was where he was made a public spectacle, Jesus triumphed over sin and all the powers of darkness (Colossians 2:15). Jesus did a complete and perfect job for humanity at the cross. Choosing and accepting Jesus into one's life and forsaking sin completely erases our debt and assures humanity of eternal salvation in the kingdom of God (Romans 5:10-11).

When Adam and Eve committed sin all three aspects of humanity received negative consequences, death being amongst them. This entails both physical and spiritual death. Jesus' death at the cross was to provide humanity with spiritual eternal life. The hope and confidence of those who have given their lives to the Lord Jesus Christ is that even though their physical bodies die, their spirit being lives forever in heaven. Please read the verses in 1 Corinthians 15:35-58, then make notes on your understanding of the text.

Jesus is sometimes referred to as the bridegroom; he loves humanity so much so that He came to die at the cross to redeem His bride: all humanity, from the snares of the devil (John 3:22-31). Those who choose to accept His love and make Him their Lord and Saviour are invited to His wedding feast. It is a ROYAL WEDDING FEAST. Jesus will return to earth to collect His bride; at a time only known by God the Father. The main goal of this book is to announce the bridegroom's invitation of humanity to attend the royal wedding feast. *Then the angel said to me, "Blessed are those who are invited to the wedding supper of the Lamb!" And he added, "These are the true words of God." Revelation 19:9.*

This is such an exciting event, not to be missed by any human being. Jesus' invitation MUST be shared with humanity, as quickly as possible (Mark 16:15). Additionally, this invitation must be urgently shared to humanity, because of this insight from the Word of God: *"Woe to the earth and the sea, because the devil has come down to you with great fury, because he knows his time is short"* (Revelation 12:12). The devil is very busy in his mission of deceiving humanity so that they do not receive Christ as their Lord and Saviour, he knows that *his time is short*. Likewise, humanity must wake up; the call to accept the love of God is very urgent. Further deliberation on the royal wedding feast follows later in lesson 10.

There is no pressure, God gives humanity options from which they must choose their spirit's final destination. However, He has clearly stated the consequences of both choices. God encourages humanity to choose life, because if they do, they choose Him (God). These are some of the verses about choosing: Deuteronomy 30: 15-19; Joshua 24:15; Revelation 3:20.

Perhaps this is a good time to reflect on all the choices discussed above. Please take some time to reflect on the two options and consequences mentioned above and complete the table below:

Bible Text	Consequences of Good Choices	Consequences of Evil Choices
Deuteronomy 30: 15-19		
Joshua 24:15		
Revelation 3:20		

Which Comes First: Body, Soul or Spirit?

It is not the author's goal to speak for God, because He does this with or without humanity (Numbers 22:28; Luke 19:40). Humanity is not in charge of their spirit, God is. While health personnel continues to do a great job in providing support to those infected by the various illness; they have no control over the souls of those they care for. Numbers of people die around the globe in their care. There comes a time when they also confess that they have tried all they could and could no longer provide any further help; the person then dies. This means that the spirit put by God in the mud goes back to the provider (Ecclesiastics 12:7).

We have realised that humans are not just the body which we see; there are hidden aspects, not visible to the naked eye. While the three components of humans are interrelated, they each have diverse daily needs; which when unmet negatively impact each other and the human being as a whole. The reverse is true, if all the unique needs are well catered for humanity functions at their optimal level.

Kindly do a personal inventory and reflection on how you nourish each of the three aspects of your being and the length of time you allocate to nourish each domain. Below is a table showing the three areas of humans. Please reflect on how you have addressed the needs of each area in the past 24 hours and allocate the length of time you spent on each aspect. This means that the total time spent on all three areas will add up to 24 hours.

Time of the Day	BODY/TIME	SOUL/TIME	SPIRIT/TIME
00:00			
01:00			
02:00			
03:00			
04:00			
05:00			
06:00			
07:00			
08:00			
09:00			

10:00			
11:00			
12:00			
13:00			
14:00			
15:00			
16:00			
17:00			
18:00			
19:00			
20:00			
21:00			
22:00			
23:00			
00:00			
00:00			
01:00			
02:00	Total	Total	Total
TOTAL TIME			24 hours

You have done a fantastic job, well done. Please take some time to reflect on the process of the above exercise. How did you find the process of this exercise, you may want to look at the number of hours you spent nourishing each area? What do you think about the length of time spent on each aspect of your being?

Did you find that the needs of the body are allocated more time than the other two, in 24 hours? Yes/No

What do you think is the reason behind a disequilibrium?

Perhaps you made a similar observation to this one. When I did this exercise, I noted that in 24 hours I spent less time attending to my invisible areas (soul and spirit); only an hour. The majority of my time (23 hours) is spent attending to my physical needs, the visible me. As we have already deliberated in the previous paragraphs, a negative impact in one area has negative consequences to the other two aspects. Perhaps due to lack of knowledge, time and understanding about the importance of the other areas of humanity, one is not able to address adequately or nurture and nourish the soul and spirit.

Have a think about how you would like to balance the time spent on each of the three human domains, as a way of enhancing the optimal function of humanity and a holistic wellbeing.

Providing adequately and appropriately for each area of humanity enhances a holistic human being. On the other hand, scarce allocation of time and attention to some aspects of humanity promotes disequilibrium which in turn has a negative impact to the whole being. While there are other strategies which are and continue to be used to support the soul and the spirit, these lessons provide humanity with an opportunity to dig deep into the food of the spirit and the soul as they focus on their creator: the giver and taker of the spirit (Matthew 10:28).

Appropriate food for the spirit is an excellent strategy to promote humanity's holistic wellness, including mental well-being (Peter 5:7; John 14:27; Philippians 4:6-7). This is important because it encourages humanity to focus on God as the one and only source of the essential entities for meeting the unique needs of the soul and spirit. He qualifies to be in this position, because He is the giver of the spirit (Genesis 2:7; Ecclesiastics 12:7) and more so because He created and loves humanity; God desires to have a continuous fellowship with humanity today and forever (John 14:23; Revelation 3:20). To emphasise the importance of looking to God for the nourishment of the spirit, please refer to the analogy of the Mercedes-Benz car part replacement we talked about at the beginning of this book.

The harmonious relationship between God and humanity was interrupted in the Garden of Eden, where the devil used the serpent to manipulate their will so that they made a wrong decision: they sinned by eating the forbidden fruit. This means that their spiritual genetic formation was altered by the introduction of the sinful genetic make-up from the devil. Up to this day the consequences of sin impacts humanity in all areas of their life, including the environment/earth we live in, as stated: "cursed is the ground for your sake" Genesis 3:17. God declared that man would die, the death of the body (Genesis 3:19) and the soul/spiritual death (Ezekiel 18:20; Romans 6:23).

One may ask themselves about the death brought by sin. Even though God proclaimed that Adam and Eve would die, they lived for a number of years after the fall. This indicates that there are different types of deaths found in the Bible; physical and spiritual. When God placed humanity in the Garden of Eden His intention was for them to live forever. Even though they sinned, because of His love and grace, God postponed their **physical (mud) death,** instead he relocated them from the beautiful garden to another one where they were assigned to till the soil (Genesis 3:23). However, the dying process begun immediately and Adam's physical body finally died at the age of 930 years (Genesis 5:5). Also, their **spiritual death** was instant; Adam and Eve were immediately separated from God. They were then taken out of the garden and the garden was protected by cherubim (Genesis 3:24).

God is Interested in Humanity: They are His Asset

Satan took advantage of Eve's will; humanity's God given ability to be autonomous, that is, being able to choose between right and wrong. The devil's target was to influence Adam and Eve to take his option (fall into sin) rather than follow the instructions given by God, because he knew that would terminate the good relationship and fellowship they had with God (Isaiah 59:2).

The devil set a trap to trick humanity into sin. Sin is the very thing that separated Lucifer from God. He left the glorious place and position in heaven; now hell awaits him where he will be tortured and tormented forever. As such, his mission is to get as many people as he can to go with him to eternal destruction and he is aware that he does not have much time (Revelation 12:12). On the other hand, God paid the price to restore his relationship with humanity (John 3:16). He paid the price to rescue humanity from the snare of Lucifer (Psalms 124:6-8). It is hoped that after these lessons the reader will be able to make an informed decision about which side or path they would like to follow: God's or Satan's.

The biggest question is 'why did Jesus bother about coming to earth to die? What for? How is humanity involved in all this?' Perhaps you have asked yourself these questions and many more. Before a further deliberation on the above questions let me share this story. When one of my sons turned 16 years, he informed my husband and I that he was now independent and had the liberty to do anything that he desired. He also told us that he was now free to explore 'things' and would be returning home at any time during the night. Although we reminded him that we still expected him to adhere to the rules at home, he refused to listen, stating that he wanted to be allowed to do as he desired and to make his own decisions; as he was getting ready for adulthood.

My son did not return home until midnight, most nights. Although his father and I prayed and trusted God that He would protect our son wherever he went, my husband and I would not settle at home to wait for his return. In the cold weather his father would go out into the dark, to search for his son. Despite him not being able to find his son most nights, his father did not give up searching. You should have seen the joy and happiness on his return on some days, when he found his son, he was forever pleased that his son was finally home, safe.

While this was not a pleasant experience for my husband and I, it was worth going through, because I find it to mirror the pain experienced by God our heavenly Father when His children (humanity) are not in His house, that is, not giving God His position as father in their lives. This has fuelled our passion and desire to share the love of God to all humanity. To let humanity know about the immeasurable love found in our God, because He created humanity in the first place and is preparing a blessed eternal home/heaven for all those who choose Him (John 14:1-2). A place where all the troubles of this life will no longer exist. Humanity is invited, those who will attend are those who CHOOSE to accept Jesus Christ as their Lord and Saviour.

When God provided the consequences of deceiving his people to the snake, he stated that *"and I will put enmity between you and the women and between your offspring and hers; He will crush your head and you will strike his heel."* Genesis 3:15. God informed the snake that the seed of the women would crush his head, that he will be destroyed by the very same women he used to introduce sin into the world. I find this very comforting and encouraging; that the very weak vessel (Eve) was chosen and used by God to destroy the devil (snake) by crushing its head. While others would have only seen Eve as a disobedient child, God gave her the strength and ability to fight back the consequences of sin.

Up until today, God's mission is to restore his relationship with humanity. This He did by first sending His only son to die for the sins of humanity. He has then left humanity to choose between the devil and Himself. God's initial plan was for His spirit invested in humanity to be in charge and lead all aspects of the human being. He never intended the body to be in control, because its desires are temporal. Humanity's fall into sin gave room for the body to be in control of the whole being, including God's spirit. God commands humanity to focus on their spiritual being, a vehicle to succeed in all other aspects

36

(Matthew 6:33; 1 Timothy 4:7-8). Please read the two bible texts, make notes on your thoughts and what the verses mean to you, regarding the following:

Seeking God's kingdom first

Other things

What we are to reject

Physical versus spiritual benefits

As humanity focus on making the spiritual being to take the lead, there is always a tension, between good and evil; right and wrong. We are ever so grateful to the Holy Spirit; He is part of God's trinity. The Holy Spirit infuses inner strength into humanity, giving them the ability to fight evil, so that humanity's spiritual being takes the lead; Philippians 4:13 *"......I am ready for anything and equal to anything through Him who infuses me with inner strength and confident peace."* A further elaboration on the fight between the devil and the children of God will be done in lesson 11.

The God Given Vacuum

The disruptions of humanity's relationship with God created a vacuum within their spirit. There is no substitute for God's presence in their spirit. In an attempt to fill this vacuum humanity constantly tries many different things, but unfortunately the space remains empty. It can only be fulfilled or satisfied by the presence of God in their life; through continuous fellowship and communion with Him. In their quest to complete God's vacuum in their spirit, humanity (knowingly and/ or unknowingly) indulge in many short-term fulfilling activities, some of which are self-destructive. Please take some time to brainstorm on some of these activities and behaviours commonly used to try and bring satisfaction to the spirit. From the list made on the left side, make a note on some of the long-term consequences of engaging in these behaviours.

Unfulfilled Things/Activities/Behaviours	Long-term Consequences

Perhaps one may start small, attributing the behaviour to a social engagement or recreation. However, as time goes by, they find that they are unable to pull out of the habit, because of being addicted. This is so critical during the adolescent and teenage period when the will of humanity begins to be dominant.

Spiritual needs and desires can never be satisfied by anything other than God's presence in the life of humanity. There is endless satisfaction, comfort, hope and contentment which comes about as a result of allowing God to control the life of a human being. Those who accept his love and leadership, receive regular spiritual meals from His various sources. Please read the verses below and make notes on your understanding of some of the benefits experienced by humanity as a result of the presence of God in their life.

Psalms 16:11

Psalms 22:26

Psalms 107:9

John 6:35

John 7:38

Having worked with persons in the health industry for over twenty years, I have had an opportunity to engage with some of them on a one to one basis. There are many reasons why people attempt suicide. Some who attempted suicide have said that they lost hope to the extent of opting to take their own lives. Perhaps, after attempting to fill God's vacuum in one's life with unfulfilling things, one might lose hope and see no better way forward than ending their lives. Please take a few moments to reflect on your life. Make notes on the following:

Do you sometimes feel that there is a vacuum inside you which needs to be filled by something?

What are some of the things you have used to try and satisfy or fill the vacuum?

Have you ever thought that life is not worth living for?

Name one or two specific reasons which make you feel life is not worth living for.

If ending your life has a negative impact on your eternity, how best would you rather deal with the issues highlighted in the previous question above? For example, you might prefer to talk about it with a trustworthy friend.

A brief biblical perspective of suicide is discussed below.

No! to Suicide: Jesus is here to help

This subject is quite wide and sensitive. It is hoped that humanity will gain an insight into this subject from God's perceptive, and perhaps look unto Jesus as their source of comfort and hope for today and tomorrow. Suicide is the act of intentionally taking one's life. Which means that the individual causes self-infliction which leads to sudden death. Committing suicide is not normal, because a person normally loves their body, as stated: "*.....no one ever hated their own body, but they feed and care for their body…………*" Ephesians 5:29.

When committing suicide, one must deal with a number of sins and or die without having confessed them. I was fortunate to support one lady who had taken a very poisonous insecticide to take her life. While laying on her bed, I noticed that she was restless and she started struggling to breathe. I went to her bedside and asked what she wanted to talk about and she stated that she wanted to ask Jesus to forgive her all her sins, including the fact that she swallowed an insecticide, because she was upset by her boyfriend. She confessed with her mouth that Jesus is Lord and she asked Jesus to enter into her life. Five minutes later she took her last breath and died. From this experience I learnt that it remains a secret to know who finally enters heaven and who does not. Therefore, no one can judge or make a conclusion about who entered heaven or did not when they die. Jesus stated: *"Do not judge others, and you will not be judged"* Matthew 7:1; *"The last shall be first and the first last"* Matthew 20:16. This is not to say that committing suicide is okay. We shall see below that all the people who committed suicide in the Bible were ungodly. There are no godly people who took their lives in the Bible.

People who commit suicide seem to inform their creator that 'you have failed to help me, therefore, I quit.' This is sin, because such a person believes and acts as if they are above God. Perhaps even before getting to the conclusion of committing suicide there is an experience of emotional and spiritual tension within the individual, maybe regarding whether to commit suicide or not, continue to find solutions to the eminent problems, whether they will be accepted by God or not, and many more. According to James 4:2 unfulfilled desires leads to murder/suicide: *"You desire and do not have, so you murder."* Within the same verse God gives a solution to: *"to ask."* In Matthew 7:7-11 Jesus urges his disciples to *"Ask."* Therefore, taking one's life is not a solution, because God urges humanity to ask, especially because there is no problem too big, He cannot solve Matthew 19:26; Mark 10:27. Please read the following verses and make notes on your understanding of the content:

Proverbs 3:5

Genesis 18:14

James 1:5

Ephesian 6:4

Jeremiah 32:27

Luke 1:37

The following are some of the quotations taken from: https://biblereasons.com/suicide/

- "Suicide doesn't take away the pain, it gives it to someone else."
- "If you are looking for a sign not to kill yourself this is it."
- "If you're going through hell, keep going."
- "Never let a stumble in the road be the end of the journey."

There are six people who committed suicide in the Bible. Although Samson might be viewed as the seventh, because of different views on his death, we will only look at six. Please take some time to read the following text, then make notes on how and why the named persons took their lives:

Judges 9:54

1 Samuel 31:4

2 Samuel 17:23

1 Kings 16:18

Matthew 27:5

In conclusion, the word of God instructed humanity not to commit murder (Exodus 20:13). This means that taking one's life is sin, because such a person is committing murder to the self. Those who kill will be judged by God, as stated by Jesus in Matthew 5:21. The best option is to trust God for help at all times, even in difficult situations, because He is able to do anything, there is nothing impossible with Him, and anyone who persevere will be rescued by God in the end (Luke 1:37; Matthew 24:13). *"But Jesus looked at them and said, "With man this is impossible, but with God all things are possible."* Matthew 19:26.

The devil might find a good opportunity to torture humanity with bad thoughts during difficult times, such that the individual experience a lot of tension within themselves. They get into the battle field of the mind. Some might blame God for what they go through, this tends to cause a struggle in trusting and believing that God has a solution for every problem, even when we have sinned, God is always available to help those who call upon His name: *"Call upon me in times of trouble; I will rescue you, and you shall glorify me"* Psalm 50:15. You can call upon God right now, He is waiting to help you. Please take a moment and reflect on your difficult situation, or one which someone you know is going through. Please tell it to God as if you are telling your best friend, let God know how you would like this problem to be solved. Believe in your heart and wait patiently for His intervention. You will soon testify about the deliverance of God from this difficult, seemingly unsolvable situation.

Let us remember that before humanity fell into sin the emptiness in their spirit was completed by the presence and regular fellowship with God. In other words, their spiritual being was content by the presence and regular fellowship with God. Before Jesus' death on the cross, humanity made animal sacrifices for their atonement of sin, until Jesus was made the perfect sacrifice. So that humanity can have direct fellowship and communion with God, their creator. When they choose to accept His love, they not only enjoy fellowship while living in this world, but will enjoy continuous fellowship with God, forever (Isaiah 57:15; John 14:23; 2 Corinthians 6:16). Additionally, humanity has been invited to the royal wedding feast where there will be endless celebration and fellowship with God and our Lord Jesus Christ, the groom of the church (Revelation 19:6-9). This subject will be discussed further in subsequent lessons.

LESSON 5
The Tension Within and Without

In the second lesson of this book, we discussed about how God created the world we live in. We then specifically discussed the creation of humanity in the third lesson and how they fell into sin, after being tempted by the devil in the Garden of Eden. The devil took advantage of Eve's will; her God given ability to be autonomous: being able to choose between right and wrong. The devil's target was to influence Adam and Eve to take his option rather than follow the instructions given by God. In this lesson we will be able to reflect on what has been discussed, which will then lead us to further deliberate on Satan's strategies to attempt to continuously destroy the relationship between God and humanity. This leads to on-going tension within humanity and or their surroundings.

The Tempter's Host

To accomplish his mission: steal, kill and destroy (John 10:10), the devil uses anything and anyone; including the individual person faced with the temptation. The devil's main target is God's asset: a human being. The seed of evil was planted in humanity when Adam and Eve accepted the devil's advice. This means that up to today the 'serpentine nature' of Lucifer still continues all around the world. We live in a 'serpentine' world. The 'serpentine' world hates and hisses at humanity, with an intention to get as many as possible into hell, where he will be destroyed eternally. God's word says the devil roars around this world like a lion, looking for someone to devour (1 Peter 5:8).

The offspring of Adam and Eve was born with the seed of evil (lineage of spiritual death) introduced by Lucifer (Psalms 51:5). This is immediately revealed in the first human baby born to Adam and Eve. Please read Genesis 4:1-15. Make notes on this text and name the specific seeds noted within this narration.

Cain was the first son of Adam and Eve. Both children were brought up in a godly fashion, as revealed by their act of preparing and bringing an offering to God. You have already made notes on their story from the previous text and have enumerated some of the seeds revealed in Cain. Cain was angry at Abel, because his (Cain) sacrifice was not accepted by God. This went on for days and God warned him that this internal feeling was the devil's seed, which he (Cain) was supposed to overcome (Genesis 4:6-7). However, we are not informed about Cain's positive response, instead, in the following verse, we learn that he allowed these feelings to go on for days, until *"one day"* the fruits of the seed came alive, where he implemented his plan to kill his brother. Please make notes on your feelings about Cain's act.

It is no wonder that we see and hear evil things happening around our communities and the world: violence, wars, hatred, social injustice, and corruption, to name a few. Perhaps this reveals in a much vivid way that God has given humanity the power of the will; to either allow Satan's seed to grow in their lives or to choose God's seed to rule over their lives. Some of these occurrences are a result of the choices of humanity.

While Lucifer does not force people to host him, he persuades their will to let them be his host so that he can accomplish his mission. This means that even though God is in control he has given humanity the will to either choose Him (God) as a host (Revelation 3:20) or to be the host of Lucifer (John 8:44; 1 John 3:7-8). We will recall, from lessons 3 and 4 that the needs of the three aspects of humanity are met differently. We have also realised that spiritual needs tend to receive less attention, with more emphasis being on meeting the needs of the physical being. This leads to continual tension from within the individual. As a result of the different needs of the three aspects of humanity, there is constant war within the person (Galatians 5:17) *The natural person does not accept the things of the Spirit of God, for they are folly to him, and he is not able to understand them because they are spiritually discerned* (1 Corinthians 2:14).

Commenting on the fall of humanity, Matthew Henry stated: "*A perpetual quarrel is here commenced between the kingdom of God and the kingdom of the devil among men. It is the fruit of this enmity: that there is continual conflict between grace and corruption in the hearts of God's people; that there is a continual struggle between the wicked and the godly in this world.*" We will discuss and celebrate God's vivid victory through the death and resurrection of our Lord Jesus Christ in lesson seven.

Please read the Bible verses below and highlight some of the ways to deal with the tension between the body and the spirit.

John 3:1-3

Romans 12:1-2

Romans 6:6

James 4:7

Hebrews 2:18

We will briefly look at some of the hosts used by the devil to tempt the people of God. To tempt Adam and Eve, Lucifer used the snake (Genesis 3:1). The devil used Job's wife to persuade or tempt Job to curse God (Job 2:9). This was because Job had lost all of his riches and all his children died. Job was also infested with boils all over his body, they could not heal and as a result he sat on ashes and scraped himself with a potsherd. In Matthew 16:21 Jesus informed his disciples that He was going to suffer, die and be raised on the third day. Please read Peter's response to Jesus (one of Jesus' disciples) in Matthew 16:22. What do you think about Peter's response?

Also look at Jesus' response, after Peter's remarks in Matthew 16:23. Imagine you were Peter. How would you have felt or responded to Jesus' comment?

Closely look at the three examples above. What can you learn from the devil's mission?

What can we learn from the responses of the following, when they were approached by the hosts of the devil?

Job

Jesus

Take some time to reflect on your past experiences. Mention similar situations which you may have gone through or have heard that others have gone through; write about them and identify key elements and how best the host of the situation was or could have been dealt.

Situation

Key elements

Best way of dealing with the situation

Situation

Key elements

Best way of dealing with the situation

Situation

Key elements

Best way of dealing with the situation

There are a number of lessons I learnt from Jesus' response to the host (Peter), three are outstanding. First Jesus shows us that it is important to know God's purpose for one's life and their destination. It might have been easy to view Peter as one on Jesus' side, trying to protect him from harm. Yet the devil was behind Peter, with the motive to stop Jesus from going to the cross, where humanity's relationship with God would be re-instated. Jesus was very wise; he confronted the enemy in Peter and not Peter. In other words, Jesus was able to make a clear distinction between Peter and his enemy.

Secondly, as a follower of Jesus it is paramount to read, know and live by God's word (Matthew 4:4). Initially, Peter was aware and he actually confessed that Jesus is the son of the living God (Matthew 16:13) who would come to the earth to deliver humanity from their sin. However, when Jesus mentioned that the time was drawing nearer for Him to die and be raised again, Peter did not remember Jesus' mission. Perhaps Peter also looked at the benefits he would lose when Jesus was no longer with them, for example walking on the water, getting free fish and loaves of bread, healing of his mother in law, to name a few.

The third lesson is also a prayer item; that I will always be spiritually awake to realise the tactics of the devil when he wants to make me a host. To always choose Jesus and make Him in charge of my life, so that the devil will not have room in my life (Ephesians 4:27). The Holy Spirit is very wise; He helps humanity to be aware of the tactics of the devil and He enables them to resist the devil (1 John 4:1). God has promised that if we resist the devil he goes away, as long as we submit ourselves to God (James 4:7).

It is easy to blame Adam and Eve for listening to the devil, because we would not be where we are today, bearing the consequences of sin: death. Perhaps one could also argue that the consequences of sin should have only been bore by Adam and Eve, because the rest of humanity were never part of their wrong decision. Unfortunately, sin entered the world through one man and this way death. Therefore, all the consequences entered humanity: through the sin of one person (Romans 5:12). All humanity has sinned, from birth and are only rescued by the love of God (Romans 3:23; Psalm 51:5; 1 John 1:8).

We are ever so grateful that our heavenly Father and creator brought a permanent, perfect solution and reversal to the devil's plans, through the death and resurrection of the Lord Jesus Christ. *"Therefore, as sin entered this world through one man, so did salvation from the consequences of sin. We now have eternal salvation through one man, our Lord Jesus Christ's death and resurrection"* Romans 5:19. Kindly make notes below, on what the above verse means to you.

We have already talked about the fact that only one aspect of the human being is visible, the body. It is also temporal. The soul and spirit are invisible, yet live forever. Within this lesson we also discussed how humanity fell into sin and now they must die. It is so comforting to know that this is not the end of the story, but the beginning of the evidence of God's unconditional love. Soon after their fall God revealed His plan of salvation for His precious asset. In fact, it was after the fall of humanity that God first announced His plan of salvation for His beloved humanity. As a consequence of deceiving humanity God informed the devil that *"......I will put enmity between you and the women, and between your seed and her seed. Her offspring will crush your head, and you will bite her offspring's heel"* Genesis 3:15. Please enumerate your thoughts and feelings as you read and think about the above verse.

LESSON 6
There is No Substitute for God

We are now aware that the human body is temporal, the spirit and soul lives forever. In lesson 4 we briefly talked about the God given vacuum in the life of humanity. In this lesson we will discuss the fact that God has no substitute in the life of humanity as stated in Acts 4:12; and Psalms 18:20-25 *"God made my life complete when I placed all the pieces before him. When I got my act together, he gave me a fresh start. Now I'm alert to God's ways; I don't take God for granted. Every day I review the ways he works; I try not to miss a trick. I feel put back together, and I'm watching my step. God rewrote the text of my life when I opened the book of my heart to his eyes. The good people taste your goodness, the whole people taste your health..."* We will briefly look into the spiritual journeys of two kings from the Old Testament: Saul and David. A final discussion will be made on the importance of having a God separated relationship.

King Saul

For a long time, Israel had no king, they were led by God under the authority of prophets. When prophet Samuel became old the Israelites demanded a king, because they felt that Samuel's sons were not following his father's footsteps (1 Samuel 8:1-4). King Saul was the first king of Israel; he was from the tribe of Benjamin and was anointed by the prophet Samuel (1 Samuel 9:27; 10:1). Even though he started his journey very well, he did not end it the same. King Saul made wrong choices in his leadership and God was displeased. The seed of the devil was manifested and he became rebellious against God. During the last days of his life his spirit was tormented, because the Spirit of God left him. This was manifested on his physical being.

Please read the following text and make notes on the sins committed by King Saul.

1 Samuel 15:10-34

1 Samuel 28: 1-20

As already discussed in the previous lessons of this book, sin disrupts humanity's relationship with God. Saul **chose to rebel** against God's instructions, by taking spoils and sparing Agag, the king of the Amalekites. He was **stubborn and proud**. He could not acknowledge his sin on return from battle, he claimed to have performed his assignment as required, until he was confronted by prophet Samuel about the noises behind him. Saul lied to Samuel, stating that he had performed God's assignment as he commanded (1 Samuel 15:13). God considers rebellion as the sin of witchcraft and stubbornness as committing adultery (1 Samuel 15:23).

Consequently, Saul's kingship was rejected by God (1 Samuel 15:26). God informed the prophet Samuel that He rejected King Saul. The prophet Samuel then disappeared and was never seen by Saul until he died (1 Samuel 15:35). This was an unpleasant experience, which was worsened by the fact that Saul's relationship/communion with God's prophet was terminated. Saul had no spiritual support. The consequences of sin and separation from God became evident in Saul's life. After God's spirit departed from him, Saul was depressed. His advisers recommended that David played a harp for him, to hopefully help raise his spirit (1 Samuel 16:16).

Seeing that his spirit remained low and that the distress could not go away, Saul sinned, once again. God is against consulting mediums and communicating with the dead (Leviticus 19: 28-35). Saul decided to **consult** the medium, in disguise. Initially, the medium declined to bring Samuel to life, stating that this had been abolished by King Saul. However, Saul swore that the lady would never be in trouble, insisting that she brings prophet Samuel to life. After receiving God's word from prophet Samuel, Saul's spirit was devastated and he could not eat (1 Samuel 28:20). Even though David played the harp for him, Saul's spirit was not fulfilled, instead he became jealous of David, especially because of the success he had during war. On several instances Saul attempted to kill David; but David ran away. Please read 1 Samuel 19:5, 9-10, then make notes on your understanding of the text.

King David

The choices and decisions made by King Saul led him to being rejected by God, instead he received an evil spirit from which he continued to be tortured and tormented. Again, God instructed prophet Samuel to go to the house of Jesse and anoint the next king, David (1 Samuel 16:1-13). David was a shepherd boy, he worshipped God with his harp, hence he was nominated to sing for King Saul when he experienced the distressing spirit. We shall briefly look at his spiritual journey and some of the choices he made while on the throne. Please read 2 Samuel 11: 1-27 then make notes on:

Main points of the story.

How do you think being the enemy's host may lead to multiplication of sin, in an attempt to cover up previous sins.

Instead of being at war David stayed at home, perhaps isolated as was Eve in the Garden of Eden, when the devil approached her to eat the forbidden fruit. This first mistake of not going to war (while other kings were at war) gave birth to all the subsequent sins, up to the murder of Bathsheba's husband, Uriah.

Please analyse David's response to God's message delivered by prophet Nathan in 2 Samuel 12:1-15.

Following their fall into sin both David and Saul experienced moments of distress, which also had negative impacts to their emotions: they lost appetite for food. This is one example where we vividly realise the link between the body, soul and spirit. Please read 2 Samuel 12:15-23. Make notes on what you learn from David's reactions to his distress before and after the death of his son.

There are several lessons to learn from the journeys of the two kings, in terms of their relationship with God. We have already discussed how humanity's relationship with God was interrupted and how their spiritual being influenced the other two aspects of humanity. The relationship between God and each of these kings influenced their decision making, especially during times of trials and temptations. An important note is that both kings initially received God's Spirit; one was left by Him and the other succeeded in all he did, because the Lord's Spirit was with him (1 Samuel 16:14; 1 Samuel 18:14; 28-29).

A. Even though he was tempted and fell into sin, David's priority was to have and maintain a clean and pure relationship with God, throughout his life journey. This is evident in his Psalms 51:10-11 *"Create in me a clean heart, O God, and renew a steadfast spirit within me. Do not cast me away from Your presence, and do not take Your Holy Spirit from me."* David chose to confess his sin to God, yet Saul chose to walk away from God: he turned his back against God and never returned (2 Samuel 13-14; 1 Samuel 15:11).

B. Instead of pleasing God, Saul's focus was making his people happy, to such an extent that he disobeyed God's command, he spared some of the Amalekites. He stated that he took spoils and spared Agag, because the people told him to (1 Samuel 15:24). On the contrary, when God's people were faced with Goliath, the giant, David's choice and decision to face him was based on his previous experience and his relationship with God, and not what the people advocated. When he volunteered to fight Goliath, David was reprimanded and ridiculed by his elder brothers, accusing him of being proud (1 Samuel 17:28, 29). He was later given an armour to fight with (1 Samuel 17:38-39), and he declined, stating: *"The Lord who delivered me from the paw of the lion and from the paw of the bear, he will deliver me from the hand of this Philistine."* 1 Samuel 17:37.

C. David wrote the book of Psalms, a true indication that his priority was on pleasing and worshipping God; making him the centre of his life. It is no wonder God declares that David was the man after his heart, twice: *"The Lord has sort for himself a man after his own heart"* 1 Samuel 13:11; *"I have found David the son of Jesse, a man after my own heart, who will do my will"*; Acts 13:22.

D. In another Psalm David sang: *"I say to the Lord 'You are my Lord; I have no good apart from you'"* Psalms 16:2.

The success, favour and prosperity comes about when humanity puts their relationship with God at the centre of their lives. This restored relationship pleases God and he can confidently declare that we are people after his heart. Humanity's goal must be to worship the one and only living God, as they travel through this life's journey. Saul's desire was to please man and his decisions were influenced by his zeal to make his people happy, rather than be influenced by God's guidance. This is a lesson to humanity today, that they must refuse to be worshipped, because God is the one and true God who is to be worshipped and he has clearly stated that he will not share his glory with anyone (Isaiah 42:8).

Vanity of Vanity: Chasing the wind

King Solomon succeeded King David. He was the wisest and richest man that has ever lived. In the previous paragraphs we discussed that God's position in humanity's life can never be substituted by anything, even though there is a temptation to try and fill God's position with non-fulfilling things. Solomon explored all avenues under the sun and he confessed that all is vanity of vanity. Nothing can ever fill the vacuum in the soul of humanity. In one of his books, Solomon stated: *"Everything is wearisome beyond description. No matter how much we see, we are never satisfied. No matter how much we hear we are not content"* Ecclesiastics 1:8.

Perhaps, at first, a reader of Ecclesiastics might understand this book to convey a message of hopelessness. Yet, Solomon brings a solution to the desperate need of humanity: fulfilling their God given emptiness; which can never be satisfied by any other thing. Not only does he qualify to share such wisdom with humanity, Solomon did research and actually pursued a lot of activities, under the sun, in an attempt to find satisfaction of their soul (2 Chronicles 9:22). Solomon accumulated worth; he collected a lot of women, including those who were foreigners as his wives: seven hundred wives, princess and three hundred concubines (Ecclesiastes 5:10-11; 1 Kings 11: 3; 2 Chronicles 9:13-28).

Solomon (being the wisest and richest man that has ever lived on earth) emphasised the foolishness, uselessness and ineffectiveness of living today's life without an eternal plan or perspective. In other words, the book of Ecclesiastics triggers and stimulate humanity to deeply reason/think about their eternity. Please read Ecclesiastes 2: 1-23 and make note below, of all the things Solomon attempted in pursue for the satisfaction of his soul.

The vacuum in the spirit/soul of humanity comes about as a result of his separation from God, their fall into sin. We will refer to this empty space as **'an eternal God-humanity vacuum**.' It was created by God and he is the only one who can fill it up. After all his research and experiences, Solomon deliberated on the real strategy to fill up the vacuum. Please read Ecclesiastes 11:7-10 and make notes on this strategy.

According to Ecclesiastes 12:1-8 when must humanity remember their creator?

The Journey

Life is a journey. Before embarking on it, it is important to know the destination, if this is not clarified it is likely that one would arrive at an unplanned destination. The final destination of the physical body is the ground, from which it was taken and that of the spirit is either heaven or hell. Regarding the spiritual journey of humanity, it is important to be confident and assured about one's decision or choice regarding their final destination. This means that there is no 'in between', one is either on God's side or Lucifer's side. This decision must be made while the three aspects of humanity (spirit, body and soul) are still together.

Perhaps we can look at the preparations one embarks on when they have a long journey. Imagine you are going overseas, for a holiday. Please name the country you want to visit. Then brainstorm on the preparation you would undertake for this journey and indicate the reason for each preparation. Some things to think about are: knowledge of your destination, location, weather, visa.

The above exercise reveals the importance of proper prior planning in order to prevent panic and missing out important elements of the journey. The passport is one of the most important items needed to safely reach the desired destination. Entry to the chosen destination is immediately granted to those who hold a valid passport, but those without one are not allowed. Please take a moment to think about an experience you might have had (or any other person you have heard about) of being denied entry into a country. Make notes on:

Why entry was denied.

Feelings about the experience.

Responses of the one involved.

Lessons learnt, if any.

The above analogy concerns a preparation for a physical journey. Likewise, the spiritual being is on a journey and proper preparations for its final destination are essential, today. This will help to avoid last minute disappointments. The first step in the preparation for the spiritual journey is acknowledging that "I am a sinner in need of God's forgiveness" (Romans 3:23; John 1:8). This means that one cannot blame others for the sins they committed, because humanity has the power of the will. Also, by God's grace we confess the sins we know and are aware of. For the subsequent steps of the preparations for the spiritual journey please read the following bible texts, then make brief notes on your understanding of each step.

Secondly: 1 John 1:9

Thirdly: Romans 10:9

Fourthly: Romans 10:10

Fifth: Revelation 3:20

Sixth: Mark 16:15

Likewise, accepting Jesus Christ into one's life guarantees that individual entry into heaven: Jesus is the passport to enter heaven (John 14:6, John 3:1-21).

Your Side/Unique for the Master/Set Apart

It is very important to note that in God's standard there are only two positions for humanity to choose from: accepting Jesus Christ as Lord and Saviour guarantees one of eternal life - heaven; refusing Jesus Christ guarantees one of eternal destruction - hell. God's principle of separation goes beyond creation, it is revealed from generation to generation. He is holy and detests sin. He is a jealous God who does not want to share His relationship with any other person/god (Exodus 34:14). God wants to be the centre of the lives of all human beings, the centre of humanity. This is clearly evident in the Ten Commandments, the first one concerns humanity's relationship with him: *"You shall not have any other gods before Me"* Exodus 20:3. God is a monotheistic being. Take some time to read and reflect on the following passages of scripture, then make notes on each text to identify the common themes of all these verses.

Deuteronomy 4:35

Deuteronomy 6:4

Deuteronomy 32:39

Psalm 86:10

Isaiah 43:10-12

Isaiah 44:6

Matthew 4:10

Act 14:15

1 Corinthians 8:6

1 Corinthians 10:19-20

Ephesians 6:6

1 Timothy 2:5

All the verses above affirm that there is only one true God who must be worshipped by all human beings. He created heaven and earth and everything in it, God created humanity to have a clear relationship with them, He loves humanity. God created humanity so that together they could have everlasting communion and fellowship. The sin of disobedience disrupted humanity's relationship with God. He then provided humanity with a road map on how they are to conduct themselves as separated beings for himself; God gave them the Ten Commandments which are written in the book of Exodus 20. These are values which govern humanity's unique separated relationship with God and how they are to interact with each other: Exodus 20:1-17. Please refer to the previous text (Exodus 20:1-17) and make a list of the Ten Commandments and reflect on what each of them mean to you:

1

2

3

4

5

6

7

8

9

10

The Ten Commandments stipulate how God would like to relate with humanity and how humanity should relate with each other, in relation to His creation (Exodus 19:5-6; Deuteronomy 5:6-21). When God instructed humanity to work for six days, He clearly stated that the seventh day must be kept Holy and set apart for worshipping Him and for rest (Exodus 31: 12-14; Deuteronomy 5:12 &14). Adhering to God's commandment is an indication that humanity has confidence only in the living God and affirms that nothing competes with God in their life. God is a jealous God (Exodus 20: 3) he clearly stated that his people are to be separated from all the things of this world and not to even intermarry nor make covenants with people from a different tribe/non-believer (2 Corinthians 6:14), because His children are holy and should not be contaminated by sin (Deuteronomy 7:1-11). God's desire is that humanity be set apart/separated solely for Himself.

We have already seen his origin and the motive of Satan, the devil. He never intends good for any human being; he was once a heavenly being who disobeyed God and was too proud to ask for God's forgiveness. As a result, God has prepared for him hell, a place of torture and torment, FOREVER.

While God has prepared this place only for Lucifer, all those who choose to disobey God and follow the ways of the devil will perish with him in the eternal lake of fire. Also, those who decide not to follow neither God nor Lucifer will also perish in the lake of fire (John 3:16, James 2:14-26, Revelations 3:16). The good news is that God closed the way to hell for humanity, by sending his only son the Lord Jesus Christ to die for the sins of humanity. Jesus' death at the cross and His resurrection is the greatest price which redeemed humanity from eternal death. Humanity received eternal life and salvation from the snares of eternal death. In lesson seven we will deliberate on Christ's victory and His love shown to humanity at the cross.

LESSON 7
A Public Spectacle

In this lesson we will look at God's victory over sin (1 John 3:8); the fulfilment of His declaration in Genesis 3:15. God's love is unconditional. Even though humanity disobeyed Him, God made a perfect plan of reconciling humanity to Himself; through the death and resurrection of our Lord Jesus Christ (John 3:16). By so doing the devil was put to shame, visible to the heavens and the earth, God made him a public spectacle (Colossians 2:15). God has won the victory over sin. The serpent's (devil) head was crushed by the seed of the woman (the Lord Jesus Christ) when he died at the cross and rose victoriously from the grave on the third day. Hallelujah.

The Woman's Seed Crushed the Head of the Serpent

After eating from the Tree of Life, Adam and Eve realised that they were naked. In the evening when God visited them in the garden, they hid behind tree leaves to cover themselves up (Genesis 3:10). This was a temporal measure to cover up their ongoing problem of nakedness. Perhaps humanity continues to use temporal measures to cover up and/or try to solve problems which can ONLY be solved by God. Take a few minutes to think about some of humanity's acts used in an attempt to solve various problems, caused by sin.

God's genuine love is revealed at the cross of the Lord Jesus Christ, where He provided humanity's salvation from their sin. Jesus is spotless and righteous, yet He came to die on earth in the place for sinful humanity. In lesson 1 of this book we learnt that Jesus existed before creation as the Word, God used the Word to create all His creation (John 1:1). God sent Jesus to rescue and save humanity from the fierce snare of the devil and from eternal destruction (Isaiah 53:8). The birth of Jesus was unique; his conception was through the power of the Holy Spirit and not of man (Matthew 1:35). While on earth He lived a very humble life, supporting humanity in all aspects of their lives (body, soul and spirit). Jesus was very focused on his assignment on earth (John 9:4; John 4:34), because He was aware that he came to the world to pronounce the victory over His enemy; through His death and resurrection at the cross. In the fullness of time the people He came to save made accusation about His identity and then hung Him on the cross. Jesus was buried in the afternoon of the day of His death and He rose on the third day, while solders watched over His tomb. He could not be contained by death, because He is life (John 14:6). Please read the previous verse and name three things that Jesus declares He is, briefly state what these mean to you.

God declared the salvation of humanity when they fell into sin: *'the seed of the woman will crush your head.'* This was realised through the birth, death and resurrection of Jesus Christ, our Lord. Although He is King of kings, creator of the universe, Jesus was supernaturally born to an earthly virgin woman: Mary (Isaiah 7:14; Hebrews 2:16). God's love and grace is magnified, where He used the very weak being (woman) through which sin entered the world to give birth to the seed which crushed the head of the serpent, the devil. This is the very woman who was blamed by Adam for giving him the forbidden fruit Genesis 3:12 *"The women you gave to be with me, she gave me of the tree and I ate."*

God chose the very weak to bring a permanent solution, to eternally restore His relationship with His asset/humanity. This indicates that God never gives up on His created being, because of His grace and His unconditional and genuine love for humanity. The birth, death and resurrection of our Lord Jesus Christ stands as evidence for God's victory over sin and the powers of the devil. Humanity is saved by grace, through the blood of the Lord Jesus Christ; there is nothing they can or could have done to be saved from their sin (Ephesians 2:8-9; Titus 3:5). Please read the two texts and then write a summary of what each text means to you.

Ephesians 2:8-9

Titus 3:5

The Wisdom of God and the Foolishness of Humanity

God's plan of salvation is perfect, freely given and is available to humanity, all around the world. Salvation from sin is received in a very simple way. *'You confess with your mouth and believe in your heart that Jesus is Lord....'* (Romans 10:9-10). This is foolishness to those who are perishing (1 Corinthians 1:18), because *".... the wisdom of this world is foolishness to God. For it is written, 'He catches the wise in their own craftiness'"* (1 Corinthians 3:19). When he was deceiving humanity in the Garden of Eden, the devil made Eve to think and believe that obeying the instructions given by God concerning the forbidden fruit was foolishness, arguing that disobeying God and eating the forbidden fruit was wise, after all it was going to make them clever; because their eyes would be opened and they would be able to know good and evil, Genesis 3:4. Up until today, the devil blinds humanity (2 Corinthians 4:4), influencing them to think that the Word of God does not tell the truth and or that it is fallible. This refers to spiritual blindness, not just blindness of the naked eyes. Many times, the devil justifies his stance by using the Word of God in a wrong context: only to his benefit. We will deliberate on this further in the subsequent lessons.

I was born again during my early high school years (25 March, 1982). I remember being laughed at and ridiculed by other students for making the decision to accept Jesus Christ as my Lord and Saviour.

Through the Word of God, I realised that they were calling me all the unpleasant names because they were blinded by the devil, to think that my decision was foolishness. I was pleased to meet them in church conferences, years later; the Holy Spirit opened their eyes and they are now born again; they are Christians. This means that it is important to hold on to our faith, despite challenges brought to us by different situations or people (Psalms 62:8; Romans 5:3-5; James 1:2-4; Romans 12:12). Please take a moment and think about some of the unpleasant statements, comments and/or names given to Christians by those who ridicule them for being born again. Write them on the space provided.

Based on the first paragraph at the beginning of this section, please make notes on your understanding and reflection on the following:

What are some of the indicators which show that the spiritual eyes of humanity are blinded by the devil (2 Corinthians 4:4)?

Name some examples of situations where humanity believes that they are wiser than God (1 Corinthian 3:19).

State some examples which shows you that God is wiser than the wisdom of this world (1 Corinthians 1:18).

What do you think about the plan of God for the salvation of humanity (Romans 10:9-10).

His Heel Bitten

Jesus suffered many things while on earth, doing the work of His Father. The journey of humanity's redemption at the cross was not an easy one. Jesus went through a number of trials and tribulations, where He was severely tortured. All these sufferings were influenced by Satan, he used various hosts in his attempt to stop Jesus from going to the cross. The devil's motive was to prevent or stop God's plan of salvation, so that Jesus would sin against God and not die to save humanity. Even though the devil's intention was to get rid of Jesus by killing him at the cross, God's perfect plan of salvation came to fruition. Jesus made Satan a public spectacle: He disarmed him from all his powers and principalities and made him (the devil) a laughing stock (Colossians 2:15).

Below are the verses narrating the suffering and death of our Lord Jesus Christ. Please read the bible text and make notes on a **brief description** of the event on each of the text. You may also indicate **your thoughts and feelings** as you read through each text.

Matthew 26: 1-5

Matthew 26: 6-13

Matthew 26: 14-16

Matthew 26: 17-25

Matthew 26: 26-30

Matthew 26: 31-35

Matthew 26: 36-46

Matthew 26: 47-56

Matthew 26: 57-68

Matthew 26: 69-75

Matthew 27: 1-2

Matthew 27: 3-10

Matthew 27: 11-13

Matthew 27: 15-23

Matthew 27: 27-31

Matthew 27: 32-44

Matthew 27: 45-56

Matthew 27: 57-61

Matthew 27: 62-66

Matthew 28: 11-15

After the fall of humanity into sin God informed the serpent that "...
you will bite her offspring's heel" Genesis 3:15. From the time He was
born, Jesus experienced a number of challenges (the devil's heel bites).
They could have stopped Him from accomplishing His God given

assignment. However, God's perfect plan remained victorious. Please read the bible text listed below, then identify any events/situations you believe to be the devil's strategy of biting Jesus' heel (the seed of the woman).

Bible Text	Biting the Women's Heel	The Victory
Matthew 1:19		
Matthew 2:1-15		
Luke 2:1-5		
Matthew 4:1-11		
Luke 4:28-29		
Matthew 14:16-22		
Luke 22:41-46		
John 18:10-11		
Mark 2:13-17		
Matthew 25:57-68		
Matthew 26:69-75		
Matthew 27:38		
John 18:39-40		
John 19:1-2		
Matthew 28:11-15		

Yet He Won the Victory

We have already realised that the Lord Jesus Christ deserves sovereign worship and adoration. Jesus did not have to die for humanity, they were responsible for their disobedience to God, but He humbled himself and took the form of a man, to reconcile His relationship with humanity. The death of Jesus cancelled the sins of humanity (2 Corinthians 5: 18, 19). By sending our Lord Jesus God reached out to earth to bring back His asset to Himself. Jesus' cross removed humanity's path to hell. In other words, the road to hell was closed for humanity, they do not need to follow this path. However, humanity has the will power to choose the path they want to pursue. There are consequences for either choice. Those who choose the cross receive eternal life and those who follow the devil's path receive eternal destruction (John 3:16).

While in this world Jesus conquered so many obstacles (Satan's heel strikes). The enemy's strikes started from the time of his birth up to his resurrections. God preserved Jesus while in his mother's womb. Perhaps Mary could have not survived her pregnancy had Joseph secretly divorced her, as he had decided when he learnt that she was pregnant. God sent an angel to speak with Joseph. The 90 miles journey form Nazareth to Bethlehem predisposed Mary to premature labour, but God preserved Jesus in Mary's womb, until He was safely delivered. At the time of His arrival in Bethlehem all rooms were filled, Mary delivered her baby in a manger.

Herod's discovery that a King was born, through the wise men, led to the death of many newly born baby boys. Meanwhile, Herod could not kill Jesus, because the owner of the universe instructed Mary and Joseph to flee to Egypt, where they lived until the death of King Herod. At the beginning of his assignment, Jesus was tempted by the devil, he wanted to stop him from going to the cross. Jesus was rejected in His home town (Nazareth) when preaching at the synagogue, they dragged Him to a cliff, attempted to throw Him over, but he passed in their midst and walked away. We have already discussed Peter's reaction and response to the news that Jesus was going to die, Jesus realised that it was not Peter speaking, but the devil trying to stop him from going to the cross.

Even though He came for sinners, Jesus was accused by many religious leaders, because they did not understand His mission. For example, they accused Him of eating with sinners and helping those in need during the Sabbath. Jesus was strongly distressed and overwhelmed by His assignment as the days of his crucifixion drew nearer, His sweat became like droplets of blood. He initially prayed that God could remove this assignment, but quickly asked for God's will to be done instead of His. While Peter thought that he was trying to help Jesus by cutting his enemy's ear, with love Jesus fixed the ear, knowing that He was not fighting against flesh and blood. Jesus bore the beating from the very people He helped. The priests, scribes, pharisees and soldiers were involved in perpetrating that Jesus be hung at the cross (Matthew 27:26; Luke 23:22-24).

Jesus was made to carry His cross, until His accusers instructed Simon from Cyrene to carry the cross (Matthew 27:32). Jesus did not deserve all this suffering He had done nothing wrong. Instead of arguing that He was innocent, Jesus kept quiet up to His crucifixion on the cross, because He was aware that the cross was the completion of the redemption plan of God's asset. **Jesus' seven statements** at the cross continues to reveal His passion for completing the plan of salvation. Take some time to read the texts below and make notes on what each of Jesus' statement means to you, mainly focusing on what we can learn about Jesus' selfless love and the completion of His Father's assignment.

1. *"Father forgive them for they know not what they do"* Luke 23:34.

2. *"Today you will be with me you will be with me in paradise"* Luke 23:39-43.

3. *"Woman, behold your son"* John 19:26.

4. *"My God, my God, why have thou forsaken me"* Matthew 27:46.

4. *"I thirst"* John 19:28.

5. *"It is finished"* John 19:30.

6. *"Father unto your hands I commend my spirit"* Luke 23.

Jesus' seven last statements confirm His triumph over sin and the wicked plans of the devil against humanity. They also reflect His unconditional love for those He came to save. Jesus' advocacy role is seen when He pleaded with His Father to forgive those who persecuted and hung Him on the cross. He affirmed His mission for coming into the world: the forgiveness of the sins of humanity. It is amazing to realise that the grace of God abounds, even up to the last moment of humanity's life, as long as they choose to accept His love. One of the criminals (on the left side of Jesus) blasphemed and ridiculed Jesus; he ended up in Hades. Meanwhile, the criminal on Jesus' right side chose to accept Jesus' love and he entered paradise with Jesus, later on that day. It's all about one's choice, God will never force anyone to accept His love. We realise that the devil never stops influencing humanity's will, persuading them to denounce God in order to choose him instead.

Please read Luke 23:39. Take some time and think about these words, imagine that these words were said to you, as you went through a very difficult situation. How would you have reacted, make some notes on your feelings and how you could have responded to the comment made by the criminal.

Even in His suffering, Jesus revealed that He is not only loving and caring for others, but that He is responsible and adhered to the law. As Mary's first-born son Jesus was aware that He would no longer be able to take care of His mother. On His third statement, Jesus assigned His brother John to take care of His mother. For the first time God turned His face away from Jesus, because of the sins of the world He carried at the cross: He was forsaken by God. As a result, He cried out loud, Jesus experienced the pain of spiritual separation from God. Jesus was sinless, yet He was punished for the sins of the sinful (2 Corinthians 5:21). Jesus' cry for water, during His last moments of life, indicated that He suffered as a human being and that He experienced physical needs.

"It is finished" is Jesus' sixth statement. Firstly, Jesus announced his victory for completing His assignment; humanity is completely saved at the cross. Previously humanity had to sacrifice specified animals for the forgiveness/atonement of their sins. Likewise, in order to escape the angel of death, just before their departure from bondage, the Israelites smeared animal blood on their door post. Hence the celebration of Passover (Exodus 12). Jesus is the perfect sacrifice, perfectly suitable to atone the sins of the world (Hebrew 10: 14-18).

Hence, on the last supper Jesus instructed His disciples to break bread and drink wine, in remembrance of Him, because He is the perfect sacrifice by whom all humanity is saved (Luke 22:19).

Secondly, when He proclaimed that *"it is finished"* Jesus announced that the devil has been defeated; that He has won the victory (1 John 3: 8). Also, by declaring that *"it is finished"* Jesus implied that the prophecy which was previously announced in the Old Testament was fulfilled (Isaiah 7:14; Isaiah 9:5; Isaiah 53:5). Lastly, Jesus proclaimed *"it is finished"* to declare the end of His suffering on earth, He was no longer going to experience the limitations and restrictions of being a human being and living among the worldly limitations and restrictions. In Jesus' final statement He surrendered His spirit to His Father. Jesus' last statement indicates that his death on the cross was not by force, Jesus actually chose to die for humanity (John 10:17, 18) hence when He had completed His desired mission, He deliberately handed over His spirit to His Father, and He died. Even though His accusers attempted to kill Him, He wouldn't let them do it prematurely, until His work on earth was completed.

During the period of His death Jesus went to Hades (the world of the death) to take the keys of life and death (Revelation 1:18), He is in control of life and death, even today. As such, humanity does not need to fear death, nor the future, because Jesus holds the keys. "He has sovereign dominion in and over the invisible world" (Matthew's commentary). Jesus, arose on the third day, but Lucifer did not give up. He bribed the soldiers who kept guard of his tomb, so that they were to spread false information: that the body of Jesus was stolen by His disciples and that He did not rise from the death. Glory be to the highest God, Jesus arose, not just Him, but other people who had died (Matthew 27:52, 53). After His resurrection Jesus lived on earth for 40 days, was seen by many, several times before He ascended to heaven. HALELUAH (Acts 1:3).

The Old Testament is loaded with God's compassion and evidence to show that His mission is to have humanity reconciled to Himself through repentance and forgiveness from sin, through the blood of Jesus Christ, His only son.   After the Israelites had sinned God proclaimed at Mount Sinai that He is *"merciful and gracious, slow to anger, and abounding in steadfast love and faithfulness......forgiving iniquity and transgression and sin!"* (Exodus 34:6-7). The stories, preaching and illustrations of our Lord Jesus are loaded with the themes of repentance and forgiveness of sin in the New Testament (Luke 3:33; Matthew 3:7-8; Acts 13:24; 19:4; John 3:16). There might be reasons why you think you do not deserve to be forgiven your sins; or perhaps you have heard others state the reasons that they believe God would not forgive their sins. Please take some time to reflect on these and make notes below.

Please cross off all the above, with a red pen or maker, because the blood of Jesus washes away ALL sins of humanity: *"If we walk in the light as He is in the light, we have fellowship with one another, and the blood of Jesus Christ His Son cleanses us from all sin"* 1 John 1:17. Jesus is the only Saviour of the world, the only one who rose from the dead and ascended back to heaven, while being watched by His disciples (Acts 1:9-12). Today He is seated at the right hand of God, interceding for those who choose Him as their Lord and Saviour, that they conquer as He did. Jesus is not only preparing their place for eternal rest (Luke 29:69; Romans 8:34; John 14:1-3) but He is also getting ready to return to earth and take His bride to His wedding feast (John 3:29; Revelation 21:2; Revelation 22:17). Jesus' resurrection is another reason for humanity's triumph/victory over sin and all the powers of Lucifer. His resurrection makes Christianity unique, it brings hope for the soul and spirit of humanity; so that, whether we live or die it is still okay (Philippians 1:21). Moreover, we wait eagerly for the return of our Lord Jesus Christ, to take us home, where His bride will never part from the groom (Philippians 3:20).

Those who choose to receive Jesus into their hearts accept God's unconditional love and their relationship and fellowship with God is restored. Their names are written in the Book of Life, and they become Jesus' bride. One day, only known by God, Jesus will return to earth; first to collect His bride, then as a judge of the world (Matthew 25:31-46; John 14:1-3; Acts 17:31). Those who choose Jesus are known by a number of names, such as: *"the bride"* 2 Corinthians 11:2. As such, Jesus died for humanity, so that those who accept His love are referred to as His bride. Jesus, as the groom, is inviting humanity to His marriage feast, where He will dinner with His bride in heaven, at the wedding feast. A detailed deliberation into this subject follows in lesson 10 of this book. Please read the following text and identify other names given to those who accept Jesus as their Lord and Saviour.

Acts 11:26; Acts 26:28; 1 Peter 4:16

Acts 18:27

Ephesians 1:1

Revelation 17:6

2 Corinthians 6:15

Colossians 3:12

My Relationship with God

From the beginning of time God desires to have a continuous relationship and fellowship with humanity; His creation, image and asset. God created humanity with His hands and He put a big part of Himself into them, His spirit and that is what makes humanity a living being. God placed humanity in the beautiful world He created, declaring that they should be in charge and overcome the world. God blessed them, instructed them to be fruitful and multiply. He is God and there is no other, His plans, will and desires will never be stopped by anything.

DO YOU KNOW HIM

You are so important to God;

He's been pursuing you since the day you were born

The bible says my King is a seven-way King.

He's the King of the Jews, that's a Racial King.

He's the King of Israel-that's a Nation King.

He's the King of Righteousness.

He is the King of Ages.

He is the king of Heaven.

He is the King of Glory.

He is the King of kings and He is the LORD of lords. That's my King......do you know Him?

David said, 'the heavens declare the glory of God and the firmament showeth His handiwork my King is a Sovereign King-no means can define His limitless love,

No far-seeing telescope can bring into visibility the coastline of His shoreless supplies.

No barrier can hinder Him form pouring out His blessings.

He is Enduringly Strong.

He is Entirely Sincere.

He is Eternally steadfast.
He is Immortally Graceful.
He is Imperially powerful.
He is Impartially Merciful….
Do you know Him?
He's the greatest phenomenon that has ever crossed the horizon of this world
He is God's Son.
He's the sinner's Saviour.

He stands in the solitude of Himself.
He's august and He is unique.
He's unparalleled.
He's unprecedented.
He's the loftiest idea in literature.
He's the highest personality in philosophy.
He is the supreme problem in higher criticism.
He's the fundamental doctrine of true theology.
He is the core and necessity of spiritual religion.
He's the miracle of the age, yes He is.
He's the superlative of earthing good that you choose to call Him.

He's the only one qualified to be an All
Sufficient Saviour…..do you know Him?
He supplies strength for the weak.
He's available for the tempted and the tried.
He sympathises and He saves.
He strengthens and sustains.
He guards and He guides.
He heals the sick. He cleanses the leper.
He forgives sinner. He discharges debtors.
He delivers the captives. He defends the feeble.
He blesses the young.
He serves the unfortunate.

He regards the aged.
He rewards the diligent and He beautifies the meek
......do you know Him? This is my King
He is the King!
He is the Key of Knowledge.
He's the Wellspring of Wisdom.
He's the Pathway of Peace.
He's Roadway of Righteousness.
He's the Highway of Holiness.
He's the Gateway of Glory......Do you know Him?
His office is manifold.
His promise is sure. His life is matchless.
His goodness is limitless.
His mercy is everlasting.
His Love never changes.

His word is enough. His grace is sufficient.
His reign is righteous, and His yoke is easy and
His burden is light. I wish I could describe Him to you.
But He's indescribable – Yes He is!
He is God.
He's incomprehensible. He's invincible.
He's irresistible.
You can't get Him out of your mind.
You can't get Him off your hand.
You can't outlive Him, and you can't live without Him.
Well, the Pharisees couldn't stand Him, but they found out they couldn't stop Him.

Pilate couldn't find any fault in Him.
The witnesses couldn't get their testimonies to agree.
Herod couldn't kill Him.
That's my King! That's my King! Yea!

And thine is the Kingdom, and the power

And the glory forever and ever, and ever and ever, and ever and ever how long is that?

And ever, and ever and ever.

And when you get through with all the

Written by Dr S.M. Lockridge

Please take some time and reflect on the poem then make notes on your feelings and thoughts about:

God's sovereignty.

Why would you choose God instead of the devil?

You can memorise the above poem, if you are able. God's word is infallible: whatever He says will come to pass (Nehemiah 23:19). God loves humanity, they are His treasure, asset, image, talented, uniquely creation, to name a few. Humanity is fearful and wonderfully made (Psalms 139:14). While Satan interrupted God's plan and relationship with humanity, this brought about a great testimony of the magnitude of the love of God for humanity: *"while we were yet sinners, Christ died for us"* Romans 5:8.

Reflecting on My Choice

On their own, humanity cannot resist/win against the temptations and strikes of the devil. The devil tempts humanity every day, every moment of their lives, even at the point of physical death. His motive is to disrupt humanity's relationship with God so that they (humanity) will not attend the wedding feast prepared for them in heaven. God has a great plan of salvation for anyone who chooses to accept Jesus as their Lord and Saviour. The first step is to confess sin, then allow Jesus to enter their hearts (become in charge of their lives). He will eat with such a person and sleep with them (Revelation 3:20). If you would like to accept Jesus into your heart you can say the following prayer; confess with your mouth and believe with your heart that He has forgiven you all your sins and you will be saved (Romans 10:9-10).

Dear Lord Jesus, thank you very much for dying for me at the cross.

I am very sorry for the sins I have committed, please forgive me.

I now realise that you love me unconditionally and from now onwards

I choose to accept you and your love. Please come into my heart.

With your help I will live a life controlled by you Jesus,

until you return to take me with you, to the wedding feast.

Thank you very much Lord Jesus for forgiving my sins and the new life in you Jesus.

Thank you. Amen.

Endless Victory from the Cross

CONGRATULATIONS for making such a wonderful decision; choosing to accept Jesus as your Lord and Saviour. There is so much joy and excitement in heaven for your salvation (Luke 15:10). Your spirit is now insured and your name is written in the Lamb's Book of Life. The sinful nature has been washed by the blood of Jesus; you now have the royal blood. God has endless blessings for those who accept Jesus as their Lord and Saviour. These blessings are received today, while living in this world and many more continue through eternity.

Before we spend some time thinking about the eternal end in the next lesson, let us enumerate some of the bonuses to which humanity has a privilege to receive, as a result of Jesus' death and resurrection. Please read the following bible text and identify some of the benefits received by humanity as a result of the restored relationship with God; through the cross of Jesus Christ. These benefits or blessings are important because they help humanity realise their identity with our Lord Jesus Christ. Please indicate which aspect of humanity each benefit addresses: the body, soul and spirit.

Bible Text	Benefits	Category: Body/Soul/Spirit
Jeremiah 17:14		
James 5: 6, 14-15		
Jeremiah 29:11		
Exodus 15:26		
Exodus 23:25		
Isaiah 41:10		
Isaiah 53:4-5		
Jeremiah 30:17		
Deuteronomy 32:39		
2 Chronicles 7:14-15		
Isaiah 38:16-17		
Isaiah 57:18-19		
Jeremiah 33:6		
3 John 1:2		

Philippians 4:19		
Revelation 21:4		
Proverbs 4:20-22		
John 14:27		
Proverbs 17:12		
Ecclesiastics 3:1-8		
Isaiah 33:2		
1 Corinthians 10:13		
1 Peter 2:24		
Matthew 11:28-30		
Isaiah 40: 29		
Psalms 107:19-21		
Psalms 30: 2		
Psalms 103: 2-4		
Psalms 6:2		
Psalms 41: 2-4		
Psalms 147:3		
Psalms 23		
Psalms 30:10-11		

Psalms 73:26		
Psalms 119:11		
John 1:12		
John 3:16		
Romans 10: 9, 13		
1 John 1:9		
Romans 3:22-23		
Romans 5:8		
Romans 6:23		
Ephesians 2:8		
Ephesians 1:7		
Acts 16:30		
John 14:6		
Galatians 5:1		
Titus 3:5		
Acts 2:32		
John 3:18		
Hebrews 9:22		
Proverbs 3:5-6		
Acts 4:12		
John 5:24		
2 Corinthians 5:21		
John 11:25		

1 Peter 2:24		
Ephesians 2:10		
John 1:12		
Galatians 5:1		
James 1:5		
Revelation 19:9		
Deuteronomy 20:4		
1 Corinthians 15:57		

LESSON 8
Mull Over the Beginning of Eternity

We have already discussed the beginning of the earth and how humanity was created; their assignment on the earth created by God. We have also discussed how sin interrupted humanity's relationship with God, their creator. In the previous chapter we elaborated on God's accomplished plan of restoring His relationship with humanity and His victory over Satan's plan. God eternally reconciled humanity back to Himself and no one can annul His victory over the devil. Eternal death of humanity came about as a consequence of disobeying God's command not to touch or eat from The Tree of Life. Even though we sinned by disobeying God and listening to the devil, because of His unfailing love and grace, God made a plan of salvation, a perfect plan to restore the initial relationship with humanity. Within this lesson we will have an opportunity to think and rethink about the end of this temporal life and the beginning of the spiritual eternal end (life or death). We will discuss the two destinations of the spirit: heaven and hell. We will then deliberate on the attributes of those who will enter each of these locations. God desires that humanity think and seriously rethink about their eternal destination.

"O that they were wise, that they understood this, that they would consider their latter end!" Deuteronomy 32:29

Humans Are Eternal Beings

This present life is only but the beginning of the eternal life to come. The previous lesson elaborated on how God sent His only begotten son to die at the cross; Jesus took the keys of Hades and death from the hands of the devil, resurrected victoriously on the third day and today He is seated at the right hand of God interceding for humanity (Romans 8:34; Hebrews 7:23-25). This means then that those who accept Jesus as their Lord and Saviour will not die, but have eternal life. Choosing to decline the love of God means that one accepts eternal death/separation from God, in hell.

One would ask what this means, because humanity continues to die. Our fore fathers and a lot of our loved ones have passed on, they are no longer with us. In lessons two and three we talked about the three aspects of humanity: the mud (physical being), the soul and the spirit (invisible being). It is quite significant to comprehend these three aspects of our being. Our physical body is temporal. When humanity comes to the end of life the mud goes back to where it was taken (ground), but the spirit returns to the owner, God the creator. We shall remember that we talked about the soul in the previous lessons, that it entails the mind, emotions, will and feelings. Using their will humanity have an assignment to decide/choose/prepare where they would like to spend their spiritual eternity.

It is important to note that this life marks the beginning of the spiritual eternity. It is only while we are in this world, the body still attached to the soul and spirit, that we can decide the final destination of the spirit. There is no opportunity to decide one's final destination after the separation of the physical body from the soul and spirit, THE CHOICE MUST BE MADE WHILE LIVING IN THE BODY. Let us refer to what Jesus said about this. Please read Luke 16:19-31. What are your thoughts regarding the following?

Today's suffering/comfort versus eternal suffering/comfort.

According to the above text in Luke, what happens at the moment of death.

The importance of caring and supporting those in need.

What we do/react about the truth of God's love for humanity, delivered by prophets, teachers and preachers.

There are a number of discussions about this story; whether it was a mere parable or perhaps Jesus' real experience. Whichever way, there are a number of things we learn. That humanity's body is temporal, but the spirit is eternal and that it is paramount to choose one's destination while still on earth. From this story of Jesus, there is no indication to support that there is salvation of humanity after the spirit/soul is separated from humanity's body. Hebrews 9:27 states *"Every human being is appointed to die once, and then to face judgement."* Please take a moment and reflect on the above verse, then make notes on your thoughts.

Also, the type of lifestyle lived today does not necessarily predict/determine one's eternal destination; the key issue is the choice made by an individual with the message delivered by the Holy Spirit, through preachers, pastors and prophets. Within Jesus' parable we learn that there is nothing wrong with having lots of money, it is the love of it (1 Timothy 6:10). Jesus' parable teaches us the importance of supporting those in need, it is a service unto the Lord (Matthew 25:35-45). Further deliberation on God's decree on the subject of caring for others and how such acts will influence humanity's entry into the kingdom of God follows in the next lesson. Over the page is an illustration to give us a glimpse into how eternity is. The red strip at the beginning of the woollen ball illustrates the few years lived by humanity on earth. The rest of ball demonstrates the endless years in eternity. This illustration it taken from the largest ball on earth, The Ball of Twine.

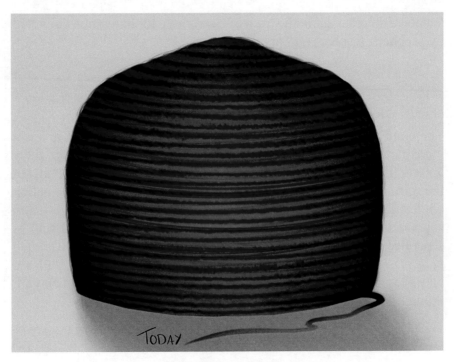

TODAY

The Endless Eternity

The world's largest ball is called The Ball of Twine, it was started by Frank Stoeber in 1953 and it is made out of a long thread. In 1961 Frank gave the ball to the Cawker City in Kansas. The one mitre red coloured section at the beginning of the ball represents the present life. The rest of the rope illustrates eternal life. The end of the rope is not visible and so is the spiritual eternity of humanity.

Humanity use their will to either choose to accepted God's love and experience a continuous relationship with Him forever; or choose to decline God's love and endlessly be without Him (Matthew 25: 34, 41). Jesus' words in John 3:16 referred to eternal death of the spirit and soul. One of humanity's critical assignments while in this world is to choose his/her desired destination for their God given spirit. Over the page is the description of each of these destinations. As one decides their eternal destination it is important to be informed about the features in each of these destinations.

Forever Without God

The primary goal for Satan is to kill, steal and destroy (John 10:10); steal humanity from God's gracious love, destroy and kill them so that they end up in hell, a place only prepared for him and his angels (Matthew 25:41; Revelation 20:10). Hell is also known as Sheol (Numbers 16:33). This is a permanent location for the souls of those who decline Jesus Christ as their Lord and Saviour. It's a place where humanity's relationship with God will never be realised, no matter how desperate and pleading they may be (Thessalonians 1:7-9). Those who end up at this destination sin against God; they pronounce that Satan is the right person to follow and not God, their creator. Hell is a place of punishment for this sin (Matthew 13:41, 50; Revelation 20:11-15; 21:8). It is important to note that rationalisation will not be relevant in this case, the only key is one's choice: accepting Jesus' Christ or declining his love. TODAY is the best time to accept Jesus into one's life and this guarantees humanity's eternal life with God (John 3:16; 3:36). Please read the texts below and make notes on what you understand to be the descriptions of hell.

Endless Punishment:

Jude 1:7

Matthew 8:12

Matthew 25:46

Revelation 14:11

Revelation 20:10

Absolute Awareness of the Agony:
Matthew 13:50

Mark 9:48

Revelation 14:10

Point of No Return
Revelation 14:11

Revelation 20:14

Revelation 20:15

Permanent Restriction

2 Thessalonians 1:8-9

Luke 16:24

Matthew 8:12

1 Peter 3:19

Revelation 20:14-15

Revelation 20:10

Forever With God

God's love and mercies are new every morning, and His faithfulness is amazing, it endures forever (1 Chronicles 16:34; Lamentations 3:22-23). Although He has prepared a beautiful place for humanity, where they will forever fellowship with Him, He still leaves humanity to choose between Him and Satan. If they choose to accept Jesus' love, make him their personal Lord and Saviour and do God's will; by His grace they will enter His eternal rest in heaven (Matthew 7:21). As you decide where you would like to spend eternity, it is worth looking and thinking more about this city.

Heaven is real, gorgeous, stunning, beautiful......

It is a beautiful dwelling place for God the Father (Psalms 33:13-14) and for those who choose Jesus as their Lord and Saviour. Jesus clearly stated that it is His Father's house and that it has many mansions, enough to accommodate all humanity John 14:1-2. At the beginning of John 14 Jesus comforted His followers, stating that their hearts should not be troubled, because of the many dwelling places/mansions available in heaven. Jesus added that He was going to prepare a place for His followers, after which He will return to take them to be with Him; forever (Acts 1:11; Thessalonians 4:13-18).

In Revelation 21:1-2 we learn that heaven is not only a real dwelling place, but it is a very beautiful and a holy city, designed and built by God (Hebrews 11:10). We alluded in the previous lessons that accepting Jesus Christ as one's personal saviour guarantees them of their entry home, in heaven. In other words, the citizenship of those who accept the Lord Jesus Christ is guaranteed in heaven. This is clearly stated in Philippians 3:20 *"But we are citizens of heaven, where the Lord Jesus Christ lives. And we are eagerly waiting for him to return as our Saviour."*

A City Beyond Cities

God is creating a new heaven and a new earth one which can never be compared to the present world (Isaiah 65:17). Please read the following texts, then make notes on the heavenly features highlighted within these verses.

Isaiah 65:18-22

Revelation 7:16

Revelation 21:2

This is a very exciting destination that no-one should miss; after all, humanity is created for this destination and there is accommodation available for all.

Heavenly Glorified Bodies

The present earthly bodies will be changed to glorious ones, please read Philippians 3:20-21. In heaven these mortal bodies are not allowed, they return to the dust from which they were taken and we will be given new eternal bodies (1Corinthians 15:35-58). Take a moment to think about some of the problems of this present body, those which confirm that it is mortal.

1 Corinthians 15: 35-58 gives a clear detailed description of the present body and the spiritual one. Please read the above verses and make notes on the following:

The nature of the resurrected body.

The difference between the present body and the new one.

The good news about the death and resurrection of Jesus Christ.

Working with the Lord, for the advancement of His kingdom.

The Soul (Emotions and Thinking)

Our God is loving, which means He has emotions. Like Him, as His children, when we get to heaven, we will have emotions and feelings. Unlike in this life, humanity experiences both unpleasant and pleasant feelings. The good news is that while we will remember the past earthly experiences; including and/or not limited to the suffering, God will wipe away all our tears, so that all pains and sorrows will be remembered no more: *"He will wipe every tear from their eyes, and there will be no more death or sorrow or crying or pain. All these things are gone forever"* (Revelation 21:4). Please take a moment to imagine the emotional state described in the above verse, make notes on your thoughts and feelings about it below. Feel free to make notes on your present emotions and feelings about any situation you might have gone through or are going through today. God loves and cares for you.

When they get to heaven, humanity's thinking will be changed. Their understanding of various things will change and all their questions will be answered; so that they will clearly understand all things (1

Corinthians 13:12). Paul was torn apart when thinking and talking about heaven. Please read Philippians 1:21-23. Make notes on your understanding of Paul's comments within the above text.

We will not miss this life; heaven is the best place to be. No adequate words can vividly explain the joy that is yet to come, when we get to heaven (Isaiah 65: 17-18; Hebrews 11:16). That is why 1 Corinthians 2:9 states *"No eye has seen, no ear has heard, and no mind has imagined what God has prepare for those who love him."* This verse gets me excited and fuels my energy to persevere in this life journey, until I reach heaven. This verse helps me to deal with feelings of disappointments and pains I experience each day, encouraging me to keep going forward to the greatest best surprise that humanity has never seen or heard. Meanwhile, I appreciate the enlightenment provided by the Holy Spirit, who helps humanity to understand and perhaps get a glimpse of the treasures in store for those who trust in Him. Thinking and pondering about heaven is very therapeutic to a lot of humans, it instils feelings of hope for the future. Thinking about heaven promotes mental wellbeing, especially as one thinks and remembers loved ones who have gone before us, that very soon we shall all be together again, forever; as David said in 2 Samuel 12:32. Please read the following verses: Isaiah 65:17-18; Hebrews 11:16.

The Greatest Reunion

What an exciting time it will be in heaven, when humanity meet together again, their eternal destination where they will never part; there will be no sickness, no fear, no pain, but endless joy, peace, love and beauty, to name a few. This is a place where one desires to see and be with our God and Jesus Christ, as well as our loved ones, so that together we will have fellowship with our God and creator, having left behind all worldly troubles and cares. Please read the following texts and point out the highlights of each text. Also make comments on your thoughts and feelings about each of them.

1 Thessalonians 4:16-18

Thoughts and feelings

2 Samuel 12:23

Thoughts and feelings

Matthew 8:11

Thoughts and feelings

1 Corinthians 13:12

Thoughts and feelings

God's desire is endless fellowship with humanity, His treasured creation. This communion with God begins while humanity is on earth, when they repent from their sins, accept Jesus Christ as their Lord and Saviour, and start living a life separated for God. When the groom returns to take His bride to heaven, there will be a lot of activities which will take place in heaven. One of the big events which will take place will be the celebration of the royal wedding feast, to welcome home the bride of Jesus Christ. We are not told how long the celebration will be, neither are we aware of the program for the wedding ceremony. Perhaps we have a glimpse of this event from the weddings conducted on earth. Nevertheless, a wedding celebration is one of the events through which the bride of Christ will be ushered into heaven. Heaven is God's magnificent dwelling place, where His fellowship with humanity continues forever/endlessly. There are a number of activities or assignments which will be done by the bride in heaven. Unlike performing duties in this world, Jesus' bride will joyfully serve God without the burden and constraints associated with working in this world. Please read the following verses then make notes on some of the bride's heavenly roles, activities and assignments.

1 Corinthians 6:2-3

1 Peter 2:9

Revelation 1:6

Revelation 7:15

Revelation 14:4

Revelation 22: 3

Revelation 14:13

Much Better Than Eden

Even though the Garden of Eden was a completely beautiful place, with beautiful vegetation, fresh flowing streams of water, it was permeable to evil. This is clearly evident by Satan's visitation and temptation to Adam and Eve (Genesis 3) and this led to the fall of man, as we have already discussed in previous lessons. According to Genesis 1 and 2 we learn that Eden was not a complete place, it was a place with great resources and potential. In other words, Eden was not a perfect place. God's instructions given to Adam and Eve in Genesis 1:28 is not only an indication of the potential in the Garden of Eden, but also shows us that Eden had a much bigger project that was to be completed *"Then God blessed them, and God said to them, "be fruitful and multiply; fill the earth and subdue it; have dominion over the fish of the sea, over the birds of the air, and over every living thing that moves on the earth."* Eden was a work in progress.

In the Garden of Eden Adam and Eve were naked, not covered with royal robes. On the contrary, in heaven we will be clothed in royal ropes (Revelation 19:8). Also, heaven is far much better than Eden. While Adam and Eve were prohibited from eating from The Tree of Life (Genesis 2:15-17), in heaven the bride will eat from The Tree of Life (Revelation 2:7).

There is no place ever known to humanity that can be compared to the life and description of Heaven's beauty. Those who have been fortunate to visit heaven and returned to earth have explained that it is very difficult to even find equivalent illustrations of the beauty in heaven for example, some of the colours seen by those who visited heaven are not available on earth to illustrate heaven's beauty. Heaven is a glorious city characterised by all good and extremely beautiful features: pleasure, joy, holiness, purity, endless delight and unspeakable peace (Revelation 7: 15-17). Unlike Eden, which is unsecure from evil, heaven is highly secure, no evil will ever enter this dwelling (Revelation 21:27).

In Eden, Adam and Eve were made a little lower than angels and yet they were made in God's image (Psalms 8:5; Genesis 1:26). However, when the groom returns to collect His bride (those who have chosen Jesus as their Lord and Saviour) they will immediately be changed to be like Him (1 John 3:2; Philippians 3:20-21). What a glorious transformation, never to be missed by any human being. This can only be realised by accepting God's invitation to the royal wedding feast.

Your Greatest Investment

Nowadays it is very difficult to trust people, because others have taken advantage of the support and help given by various donators. Other people have disguised and pretend to be living in poverty or being in need for help. Also, sometimes those assigned to distribute the allocated resources to support those in need have mismanaged the resources, diverting them to cater for either their personal gain or distributing far less (to those in need) than what was donated. As a result, those willing to help could be easily discouraged and instead ignore or reluctantly support those genuinely in need. However, the dishonesty of others does not change God's required standard and importance of helping those in need. In lesson three we talked about how God treasures humanity, despite their race or skin colour; they all have His spirit and they are His asset.

The principle of giving to those in need was first demonstrated to humanity by God; He gave humanity His only son to redeem them from eternal death. This has already been discussed in lesson seven of this book. In Luke 6:38 Jesus stated that those who want more must:

"Give and it shall be given unto you..." There are a number of benefits for supporting those in need. Please read Psalms 41:1-4, then enumerate at least seven benefits of helping those in need.

Confessing Jesus as Lord and Saviour and accepting him into one's heart is God's prerequisite for qualifying as the groom's bride (John 3:16; Romans 10:9-10). Jesus narrated an important parable in Matthew 25:31-46, one which further delineate God's criteria for humanity's entrance in heaven. Please read Matthew 25:31-46 then complete the table below.

"You did it to Me"	*"You did not do it to Me"*

During his time on earth we realise that there are a number of instances where Jesus demonstrated His holistic interest and care for humanity. For example, He looked at a large crowd of His followers with compassion and He healed those who were sick. Also, instead of sending them home hungry after a very long day Jesus prayed to His Father in heaven, five loaves of bread and two fish ended up feeding over 5000 people. More food was left over (Matthew 14:13-21). This teaches us that as we talk about feeding and supporting humanity's spiritual needs, we equally support their physically and emotionally needs, because these are all interrelated to make the complete being.

Jesus' illustration in the above text indicates that God seriously observes and records how humanity treats and supports each other, because whatever we do to any human being, we are doing it or not doing to God (Matthew 25:35). All human beings are made in God's image and are therefore His representatives. In His endeavour to support His people, God works with other human beings to support those who are temporally in need. Most of the time it may appear like one's struggle will never end, yet this is not the case. There are so many testimonies of how God elevates the 'outcasts' or those in need. For example: God used David to bring the lame Mephibosheth to live with him in the palace. David did this because of the kindness he received from Jonathan when he was in great need (2 Samuel 9:1-13). In her endeavour to help the prophet Elijah get water and something to eat, the Zarephath widow's life and that of her son was instantly changed: death could not prevail. The widow became rich from the oil provided by God through His prophet Elijah and her death was cancelled (1 Kings 17:7-16).

We have already looked at some of the attributes delineated by God for those who will be welcomed to the groom's wedding feast in lesson 8 (Matthew 25:34-46). One of the best ways to invest in God's kingdom is to help other human beings. Helping others brings great reward and positive feelings, such as the multiplication of good deeds, contentment and satisfaction. This is further fuelled by the joy of seeing others prosper and succeed (Romans 12:10; Galatians 6:9-10). The more you give, the more you receive (Luke 6:38). Please read the following verses and make notes on the highlights of each text.

Proverbs 19:17

Proverbs 21:13

Proverbs 28:27

Luke 6:38

Acts 2:45-47

Ephesians 4:32

Galatians 6:9, 10

God Uses His Children

Although this book is not about myself, please allow me to praise the Lord for all His acts of kindness. I would like to express my gratitude for the many people who have shown the love of God and kindness to my family and I. For example, when I was immobile for four months the members of the Bridge Church in Bolton (United Kingdom) showed us the love of Christ. This they did through prayer, bringing food, assisted with transport to attend hospital appointments and doing shopping. They visited me in hospital and at home and they did many other acts of kindness. I would like to assure them that this they did to our Lord Jesus Christ himself.

Also, I would like to highlight two of the most influential people in my life. Even though I am not a stranger to my parents, I would like to thank God for how they have taken and continue to care for me: Dr and Mrs Anderson Agnes Nxumalo. I am ever so proud and grateful for all the holistic support you gave me, since I was born and now you continue to show God's love and kindness to your grandchildren. Your acts of love and kindness will not fit in this book, they will be deliberated upon in another edition.

I have also seen and experienced Matthew 25:34-36 when I relocated to the United Kingdom in 2005. I always look back and stand amazed at how God took care of me through my UK mother, Mrs Edna Monica Crichton. She was used by God to make my relocation from Swaziland very smooth. When I first arrived in the United Kingdom, I lived in Watford for 8 months, then I moved to the North West. During the 8 months I attended the Elim Church in Watford, where I was warmly welcomed by a loving woman who I now call mum. At the Elim church I started serving at the Oases ministry (feeding people living in the street) and I realised that mum Monica was also involved in this ministry. A year later I learnt that mum Monica and her husband started this ministry, what a great heart to serve.

During the process of relocation to the North West my accommodation contract finished before the end of my work contract. This meant that I no longer had accommodation until my work contract had ended. As always, mum Monica asked me how I was doing and how everything was. When I informed her that I lived in the car while completing my work contract before relocating to Manchester, she joyfully invited me to live with her until the end of my contract. She welcomed a stranger. I was well accommodated in her house; I ate a good breakfast and she waited for me to return from work so we could have supper together. I managed to have a bath and had water to drink.

I sincerely appreciate all your love and support mum Monica, during my difficult time. I want to remind you mum that Jesus is saying to you ".... *inasmuch as you did it to (Siphiwe) one of the least of these My brethren, you did it to Me*" (Matthew 25:40). Thank you very much mum for all your love and support; as a stranger. Mum Monica took me in, gave me food, water to drink and she clothed me. In 2007 she travelled all the way from Watford to the North West to welcome my family, when they relocated from Swaziland. Mum Monica blessed my house, prayed over it and anointed the whole house with oil. Together we prepared a meal for my family. What a glorious moment this was. All these promoted my holistic well-being and prevented me from getting any form of distress or illness. I really appreciate God for showing me His love and guidance, by allowing this divine connection.

Mum Monica introduced me to her lovely children and grandchildren and she continues to show God's love and kindness. This is an unforgettable experience of how God used His daughter to take care of a stranger, myself. God is so faithful; he takes care of humanity as he declares *"......I will never leave you nor forsake you"* (Deuteronomy 31:6). God is ready to show you His love and goodness as you go through difficult situations, all you must do is to have faith and trust in His faithful words.

Please take some time to reflect on your experience. There could be one person to whom you would like to show God's love. Write the name of the person you would like to demonstrate God's love to. Please specify what you would like to do. Before doing this exercise, you might want to take some time to pray about this and the Holy Spirit will guide you in this exercise. As you continue with this exercise please remember what Jesus says *"......inasmuch as you did it to one of the least of these My brethren, you did it to Me"* (Matthew 25:40).

Evidence of My Chosen Destination

The Bible has clearly stipulated attributes of those who will be accepted at the royal wedding feast and those who will go to hell. Humanity can be assured today, while living on earth where they will spend eternity. The primary assurance for heaven as one's eternal destiny comes from accepting Jesus Christ as personal Lord and Saviour. Rejecting the Lord Jesus Christ indicates one's choice to spend eternity in hell. Below are verses which specify some of the attributes of those who are in heaven and those in hell, as stipulated by God.

Attributes for Destination One: Hell

Please read each of the texts below and make notes on the attributes of the individuals found in hell.

Matthew 5:22

Matthew 13:49

Matthew 25:41-46

John 3:19

John 3:36

Romans 6:23

2 Thessalonians 1:8, 9

Romans 16:17-18

Jude 1:7

Revelation 14:11

Revelation 20:10

Revelation 20:15

Revelation 21:8

Attributes for Destination Two: Heaven

Please read each of the texts below and make notes on the attributes of the individuals found in heaven.

Psalms 145:20

John 3:16

Matthew 7:13-14

Matthew 10:20

Matthew 13:49

Matthew 21-23

Matthew 25:31-40

John 14:1

Acts 14:12

Hebrews 11:16

Revelation 2:11

Revelation 20:4

Revelation 20:15

Revelation 21:7

Following the above information, please take some time to reflect, think and rethink about each of the attributes of the places discussed above. Then go through each of the identified attributes for each destination. Imagine that you have chosen heaven as your eternal destination. With the help of the Holy Spirit, see if there are any attributes which are lacking for you to qualify entry into the royal wedding feast. You may take a brief moment to talk to Jesus and ask Him to help you to maintain His correct attributes which will qualify entry into the royal wedding ceremony.

While there are a number of attributes which can hinder humanity from entering the royal wedding feast, anger and bitterness is one of the toxic sins which will be addressed in the next lesson. Perhaps this subject is important, because it is the first qualification for entering the royal wedding feast: being forgiven our sins by the Lord Jesus Christ. Jesus also informed humanity that if we do not forgive those who trespass against us, our heavenly Father will not forgive us our sins too, this means that we will not be allowed into the wedding feast (Matthew 6:14-15; Matthew 18:34-35). Please read Matthew 18:21-35 before we move to the next lesson.

LESSON 9
Confronting the Monster: Anger and Bitterness

Within this book we have already discussed how ***"Human beings are greater than the sum of their parts"*** by Aristotle. This means that a human being has more parts than the obvious physical body. They also have the soul/spirit and emotions. The purpose of this lesson is to enhance the emotional and spiritual wellness of humanity, through an emotional detoxification process; confronting and dealing with anger, bitterness and resentment. This leads to the promotion of mental and physical well-being and preventing the occurrence of physical and mental illnesses associated with chronic anger and bitterness. Also, dealing with anger and bitterness qualifies one to participate in the groom's wedding feast. *"For if you forgive men their trespasses, your heavenly Father will also forgive you. But if you don't forgive men their trespasses, neither will your Father forgive your trespasses"* (Matthew 6:14-15).

Forgiving Others: A Prerequisite

The most important qualification to enter the royal wedding feast is confessing our sins and accepting Jesus Christ into one's heart; we are then forgiven our sins and by grace we are accepted into God's kingdom. From Matthew 6:14-15 we learn that Jesus expects those who have been forgiven to forgive others, if unable to forgive then we will not be forgiven by Him.

In Matthew 5:22 we learn that harbouring anger and bitterness predisposes one to enter hell. While all the other attributes are very important, within the following lesson we will discuss issues of anger and resentment and how one can deal with such feelings. The main reason is that humanity's entry into heaven is only through the forgiveness of sin. Therefore, if God has forgiven our sins, we are also to forgive those who upset and offend us. Please read the following texts and briefly make notes on what the text means to you.

Colossians 3:13

Mark 11:25

Ephesians 4:32

Matthew 18:21-22

Matthew 6:12

Matthew 6:14-15

Definitions: Anger, Bitterness and Resentment

Anger: a strong emotional upset feeling one experiences when s/he believes to have been unfairly treated by someone or when a situation has gone wrong. Such feelings can also be directed towards the self. They can be temporal or sustained over a long period of time, even years.

Bitterness: anger and disappointment at being treatment unfairly. An ongoing process of the mind where one repeatedly replays, rethinks and relives feelings of hurt and the process which led to such experience/s. *Resentment* is a synonym for bitterness.

Signs/indications of being angry, bitter and resentful

Signs of bitterness: Generalising one's experience to a group, holding grudges, 'liking the sound of one's voice', jealous, making no change or progress, attention seeking, difficulty in accepting advice, dislike of cheerful people *(www.aconsciousethink.com)*.

Nelson Mandela stated that *"anger and resentment is like drinking poison and hoping it will kill your enemy, or the one who has created the harm in the first place. The problem is that the poison will completely destroy your mind and body over time if you let it."*

Reflection

Please make a list of some situations or experiences that could lead to anger and bitterness, for example a disagreement/conflict with a work colleague. Your list must not be less that ten (10) examples.

Anger, bitterness and resentment: physical impact

Short periods of anger are acceptable and beneficial to humanity; during this time the body enters into a state of *'fight or flight,'* a state which helps us deal with the situation. The body triggers its internal protection to either fight or flight from the situation. This is a **stressful** state of the body.

The body releases a number of *hormones*, such as cortisol and adrenaline.

The *blood pressure* increases and a *large volume of blood* moves from the hands and feet to larger muscles, in preparation for fighting or fleeing.

There is *increased perspiration* to assist the body to cool down and an increase in *platelet* adhesiveness so that the body would be able to stop bleeding, in a situation of body injury/trauma.

Digestion becomes slow or even stops and this predisposes one to constipation and cancer.

At the end of the perceived danger the body returns to its normal state of *equilibrium*, also known as a *homeostatic state*.

Ongoing or unresolved anger, bitterness and resentment places the body in a state of **continuous or chronic stress**, which leads to ongoing exhaustion, weakening of the immune system, anxiety, depression, headaches, back pain, abdominal pains, skin rashes and insomnia. This is a highly toxic state of both body and soul.

Emotional strains

In order to illustrate the impact of chronic anger, bitterness and resentment please refer to the list you formulated in the first Reflection. Imagine that from this list you have been angered by ten people and they live in different countries of the world:

Rose lives in Mexico; Brian and Ben live in Durban; Lyn and Michael live in Leeds; Elaine lives in Sydney; Ayasha lives in India and Kenneth, John and Nomsa live in New York.

Imagine that you are connected by a strong chain to each of the ten people above.

This means that you are at the centre of all ten and you move about with all ten of then tied to you, where ever you go.

Anger and bitterness provide one with an opportunity to drag around all those who offended him/her over the weeks, months, years and decades.

Even though we cannot physically see this, yet such an illustration reveals the emotional strain brought about by anger, bitterness and resentment. The emotional strain of anger, bitterness is demonstrated on the illustration on the next page.

Anger Bitterness & Resentment Emotional Toxins

Reflection

Please take some time to think and reflect on the following and make notes on your thoughts.

What are the benefits of anger?

When does anger become a danger?

How does anger and bitterness affect our bodies?

Physical detox

Definition: a process of removal of impurities/toxins in one's body, using a scientifically approved approach. A further explanation of this process is beyond the scope of this book, hence readers are advised to seek further information, if need be.

Benefits

Physical detoxification boosts energy levels. The sluggish feeling we get during the day can be the result of excess toxins in the body. The following are other benefits of detoxification: promotes good digestion and weight management; reduces body inflammation; promotes healthy skin; strengthens immune system; improves mood and makes one feel good.

Why emotional detox?

- Confronts the root of the problem and deals with it in a safe environment.
- Enhances self-introspection: identification of weakness - this promotes self-confidence.
- Enables one to confront and deal with this difficult emotional discomfort.

- Works on improving weakness: enhances progress/productivity.

- Prevents physical and mental complications as discussed previously (e.g. high blood pressure, depression).

- Provides clarity of mind versus the burden of dragging unpleasant memories of people/occurrences.

- Enhances the establishment of strong long-lasting interpersonal relationship and working well with others.

- Provides a skill which can be used on subsequent occasions needing forgiveness.

- Promotes a holistic health initiative.

Reflection

Please state if the following statements are true or false

- Physical detoxification is more important than emotional detox. (T/F)

- If one engages in emotional detox, s/he is likely to be productive is all areas of his or her life. (T/F)

- Holding grudges makes you susceptible to cold and flu. (T/F)

- Ongoing constipation and/or diarrhoea could be an indication of unresolved anger and bitterness. (T/F)

The following are actual steps one can engage in when confronting chronic anger and bitterness. It is advisable to be in a place where you can focus on the process, like a quiet place. Going through this lesson might bring about mixed and unpleasant feelings, as past experiences are relived; you might be tearful; it is ok to cry, because that is part of the healing process.

Steps of emotional detoxification

i). *Think about who/what event made you angry.* There might be several issues within this section, it is advisable to start with

ONE person/event at a time. For example: *"I am angry at my sister Rose."*

ii).   *What upset you.* At this time, you want to state the specific, this is what makes you feel angry. There may be one or several things with which you are not happy about, please state then the way you feel. For example: *"What upsets me is that she left me behind when going to the movie."*

iii).   *Why you are upset.* This step allows one to deeply explore the unpleasant situation. Using the example above: *"I am upset because we planned this trip two months ago, I allocated time to go with her now she has messed up my schedule. Also, this is not the first time she has done this to me, she is making me to look like a fool."*

Reflection

Please write, video or audio record your above answers. You might need moments of silent or could experience tearful moments during this reflection proceeds, it is okay because this is part of the healing process.

i).   *Think about how you might have made mistakes within the situation, if applicable.* Please note that this is not a self-blame moment, it is an important process of reflection which promotes self-growth and confidence. As one is aware of their mistakes and weakness, they are likely to work towards improving and avoiding subsequent occurrences.

ii).   *Write and/or video or audio record as much of the above information as you are able.*

Reflection

Decide if you really want to be free from the emotional strain of living with the anger/bitterness of your experience. If you decide that you do not want the physical and emotional strains of chronic anger and bitterness move on to the next step.

i). *Imagine a king who is also a judge, fighting your case. See him sat on the chair you brought.*

ii). *Approach him, because he is interested in vindicating for you, to report your adversary to him.*

iii). *Let the king know all which is in your heart about the situation, for example all in steps 1 to 3. You can also let him know about how you think you also contributed to the situation.*

iv). *Inform the king that you have decided to forgive......because he (king) is the best avenger for you.*

v). *Take out your coat and declare "I forgive......from doing......to me, I choose to leave him/her in your capable hands, I trust that you will do a perfect job in avenging for me.*

vi). *Think about how you are going to show kindness to......such as making a phone call, sending him or her a card.*

Reflection

This is the time to act on your proposed plan above.

Reflection and Summary

"As I walked out the door towards my freedom, I knew that if I did not leave all the anger, hatred and bitterness behind, that I would still be in prison."

Describe how you feel after going through this course, reflecting on Nelson Mandela's statement above. You might want to talk to someone about your experience, feelings and emotions. It is still okay to take some time in prayer, telling God how you feel, you can also let him know about your weaknesses and ask him for strength and wisdom. He is very much with you now and always (Joshua 1:9; Isaiah 41:10; Zephaniah 3:17; Matthew 28:20).

LESSON 10
The Royal Wedding Feast

Jesus died so that no human being go to hell. Instead He came to pay the price that humanity could not pay: saving the world from eternal death through sin. Jesus forgives all sins of humanity and as such He requires humanity to forgive each other their trespasses. Those who accept His love are called His bride, church, body, disciples, Christians, to name a few. As a bridegroom Jesus is inviting humanity to His wedding feast in heaven. In this lesson we will discuss two of His heavenly illustrations as narrated by Jesus: the parable of the wedding feast and the parable of the ten virgins. The former parable demonstrates how God's love and invitation to His feast is extended to ALL humanity; and the later emphasises the importance of being ready and alert for Jesus' return, when He will take his bride to celebrate and have fellowship with Him in heaven, forever.

The Most Magnificent Wedding

Please take some time and think about the *'most magnificent/wonderful wedding ceremony'* which you have been involved with or have seen in the past or one you would like to have or wish for someone you love. Kindly make notes on the following:

Name the bride and the groom.

Date (proposed) for the wedding.

What preparations are needed or were made.

The wedding attires: for guests, groom and bride.

The ceremony, including food.

Your feelings about the whole event.

The Royal Wedding Feast: You Are Invited

Throughout His ministry, Jesus used a number of parables (earthly story with a heavenly meaning). Within the two parables in Matthew 22 and 25 Jesus was illustrating the kingdom of God, His endless love for humanity and His expectation of how those who accept his love are to get ready for their heavenly relocation. Chapter 22 begins with the parable of the wedding feast, a narration of Jesus which is a continuation of the previous parables in chapter 21. After the authority of Jesus was challenged by the leading priests and elders, He (Jesus) narrated the parable of the evil tenant farmers (Matthew 21:32-42).

A certain landlord rented his well secured and well irrigated vineyard to tenants and he relocated to another country. The agreement was for the tenants to pay the rents with a certain percentage of their harvest. During the time of harvest the landlord sent servants to collect the rent, but they were grabbed, beaten, stoned and murdered by the farmers. The landowner sent a larger group of servants to collect the rental harvest, yet the farmers did the same thing to the servants. He then sent his own son, thinking that they would surely respect him, but they did the same. Finally, the landowner travelled to his vineyard, took all the farmers and punished them severely.

After the above parable Jesus then narrated the parable of the wedding feast. Both parables have some common features, one of which is the rejection of God's message, His prophets and Jesus Christ His son by His chosen nation; Israel. God is now raising a **righteous holy church; the body of Christ; the bride** (1 Peter 2:5). It is important to remember that Jesus' first miracle was the provision of wine at the wedding in Cana. As an inaugurator of marriages (in Eden) Jesus supplies all needs in marriages. He knows how to supply all the needs of this institution as well as maintain the initial love and joy of the couple. Please take some time and read the text below, then make notes on the main points, meaning and your understanding of its significance.

Matthew 22:1-14: The Parable of the Wedding Feast

Main points.

Understood meaning.

Importance of this parable.

In this parable we see God the Father: the king and the king's son: Jesus. The king's son is also referred as the bridegroom. The king prepared a marriage ceremony for his son. Those who accept Jesus' love are referred to as the bride. The gospel brought by Jesus Christ is the new covenant between the king, bride and the bridegroom.

The decision to change the spiritual lineage rests upon individual humans: *"But ALL who believed him and accepted him, he gave the right to become children of God"* (John 1:12). They receive a royal heritage and their names are then recorded in the royal record; The Book of Life: *"But you are not like that, for you are a chosen people. You are royal priests, a holy nation, God's very own possession. As a result, you can show others that goodness of God, for he called you out of the darkness into his wonderful light"* (1 Peter 2:9); *"All who are victorious will be clothed in white. I will never erase their names from the book of Life, but I will announce before my Father and his angels that they are mine"* (Revelation 3:5). *"And all the people who belong to this world worshipped the beast. They are the ones whose names were not written in the book of life that belongs to the Lamp who was slaughtered before the world was made"* (Revelation 13:8).

Those who choose to accept the love of Jesus are not only registered in the heavenly royal book, but are also given the right to participate in His royal wedding/marriage feast. The celebration of the marriage ceremony starts immediately when one makes this decision and continues until the bride is received in heaven. The first celebration happens in heaven; when humanity receives God's invitation to the wedding feast (accepting Jesus' love): there is a big celebration, even with the repentance of one person (Luke 15:7). Secondly, accepting Jesus into one's life opens the doorway to ALL the blessings of this new covenant, they are experienced while living in this world. **For example, the joy experienced after the forgiveness of sins; the right to be called the son/daughter of God; God's favour; peace of conscience; all the promises of the gospel; the comfort of the Holy Spirit and the unshakeable confidence of eternal life.**

Important to note is the fact that all the above benefits are spiritual experiences, their presence are beneficial and essential to the soul and spirit of every human being. The results of these are then manifest in the physical dimension of humanity, as we discussed at the beginning of this book. In other words, the presence of Jesus and the Holy Spirit in one's heart brings food and well-being to their spirit and soul. While these blessings (assets of the soul and spirit) are very essential in life today, they are not available for sale in any shop around the world, nor can they be manufactured by the best manufacturers of the world. Even if one has billions of dollars these gifts cannot be bought, because they are unique and can only be found from one source: salvation through the blood of Jesus Christ. They are free gifts for the spiritual aspect of humanity, they can only be received by accepting the love of Jesus. Please take a moment and think about these essential blessings, what do these blessings mean to you; that you are called a child of the King of Kings, for example.

In the parable of the wedding, the feast represents the kingdom of the Messiah. Those who were initially invited refers to the nation of Israel. They ignore God's servants: the prophets. As a result of Israel's rejection, God has then extended His invitation to the whole of humanity: good or bad. GOD IS INVITING AND CALLING HUMANITY TO PARTICIPATE IN JESUS' WEDDING FEAST. Those who reject God's invitation; are not worthy for His Kingdom. Instead, they confirm that their spiritual lineage is of the devil, Satan (John 3:36).

The Royal Wedding

In the parable of the wedding feast the servants were first sent to inform the invited guests that the feast was ready and that the ceremony was ready to start. The invited guests declined to attend. Perhaps, as a way of encouraging them (the guests) Jesus elaborated on the details of the preparations for the royal wedding feast. The servants returned to inform the guests that a dinner is prepared, an oxen and fatlings were killed, but the guests continued to decline the invitation. They ignored the servants and went on their ways; some to their farms, others to their businesses. Others seized the servants, insulted and killed them. God prepared the salvation of humanity a long time ago. Matthew Henry's commentary puts it very clearly that the feast has been well planned and everything is ready: *"pardon is ready, peace is ready, comfort is ready; the promises are ready, and heaven, at last, is ready to receive us."* (Page 1314, Matthew Henry's commentary, Michigan: Zondervan, 1961).

Imagine that you are the king. How would you feel about the response of your guests; how would you have reacted to their refusal to attend this big event. Also make notes on your feelings about the killing of your servants.

The royal wedding feast has been well prepared, with a young ox that was fattened to be ready for the occasion. This indicates that there is going to be a wonderful time of celebration with plenty of very nice food, there will be fellowship, laughter, unspeakable peace and joy. This is what the gospel of Jesus Christ brings to all who accept him as their personal Lord and Saviour: endless celebration. The celebration begins today, while humanity lives in this world. This kind of celebration brings heaven on earth and it continues even when Christians pass on to heaven.

Please think about a specific royal wedding you have read about or witnessed. Name it and highlight its most outstanding features.

Following their disobedience of God in the Garden of Eden, humanity does not deserve salvation, nor can they earn their salvation; they are only saved by grace. Ephesian 2:8 states: *"God saved you by his grace when you believed. And you can't take credit for this; it is a gift from God."* God's grace is amazing, because instead of perhaps giving them a position of a servant, God gives humanity the top place, being the bride to His son. Hence, those who accept God's love are the bride to the heavenly Prince, Jesus the Saviour of the world. Hallelujah!

Miss Diana Spencer lived an ordinary life and took low paying jobs while she lived in London (https://en.wikipedia.org/wiki/Diana_Princes of Wales). It was not until her marriage to Prince Charles in 1981, that she did not only became popular all over the world, but her title changed to be Princess Diana. Similarly, by accepting God's love humanity change their spiritual lineage to that of God and they then become royal, being called Princes and Princesses (1 Peter 2:9,10).

The guests in Jesus' parable do not seem to be aware about the importance of this ceremony, especially that they (the guests) are the bride. This is reflected in their reaction to the invitation; they were busy with various activities, they also ignored, ridiculed and killed the servants. What are your thoughts about contemporary humanity's response to God's invitation to the wedding ceremony of His son?

What are some of the excuses or reasons, given by humanity today, for not accepting the love of Jesus?

The Royal Wedding for All Human Race

Humanity is saved by the grace of God from their sin and not by any works or other means, for no-one can pay the price for their salvation and redemption from the wrath of God. *Salvation is not a reward for the good things we have done, so none of us can boast about it"* Ephesian 2:9. The salvation brought by our Lord Jesus Christ is available to humanity: Greek, Jews, gentiles, rich or poor (Romans 10:12). Additionally, the salvation of our Lord Jesus Christ makes humanity equal, *"There is (now no distinction in regard to salvation) neither Jew nor Greek, there is neither slave nor free, there is neither male nor female; for you (who believe) are all one in Christ Jesus (no one can claim a spiritual superiority)"* Galatians 3:28 (Amplified Bible). The love and grace of the salvation of our Lord was revealed from the beginning of creation and has been on going throughout out the history of humanity. One clear example is seen in the life of Joseph.

Joseph was a handsome young man and was admired by many women; including wives and daughters of Egyptian officials (Genesis 39:6-7). He chose to live a life of being separated for God, living a righteous life, at all times, even in a foreign land where it would have been easy to live a sinful life. This is revealed in Genesis 39:9, when Portiphar's wife asked Joseph to 'lie with her' he replied: *"How then can I do this great wickedness and sin against God?"* Please take some time to reflect on the life of Joseph regarding sexual purity. Then make notes on the following questions, especially focusing on contemporary society.

What are your thoughts and feelings regarding the choice made by Joseph, of abstaining from sexual immorality?

What are the strategies used by the devil to tempt humanity to fall into sexual impurity?

To the youth

To adults

How do you think Joseph could have reacted to 'internet sex' and why?

Perhaps there are a number of things to discuss in relation to sexual issues, which we will not be able to exhaust within this lesson. You might want to explore what the Word of God says about sexual issues. Please read the following verses then make notes in the spaces provided, as you think about what God says regarding: sex before marriage (fornication), sex with another person's wife/husband (adultery), same gender sex, polygamy versus monogamy, how to run from sexual immorality and how to deal with it.

Exodus 20:14

Leviticus 18:22

1 Corinthians 6:18-19

1 Corinthians 3:13

1 Corinthians 6:9-10

1 Corinthians 7:2

Ephesians 5:3-5

1 Thessalonians 4:3-4

Matthew 15:19

Matthew 19:9

Matthew 5:28

1 Corinthians 6:18-20

Jude 1:4

1 John 2:3-4

Hebrews 13:4

Revelation 21:8

God has clearly stated that Jesus will return to earth to take a pure Church, a virgin which has kept herself clean and undefiled by sexual immorality, because sin will not enter the royal wedding. Joseph is one of the great examples to the bride of Christ, confirming that it is possible to flee from all sexual immorality and to live a life set apart for God, despite the endless pressures of this world.

In the same way which brought Aseneth (a gentile: Egyptian woman) into the Jewish family, the royal lineage where Jesus was born; the same love and grace opened the gate of salvation from sin for all of the human race (black, white, green, yellow, red); all are equally invited to partake at the royal wedding. Through God's divine power and unmerited favour Aseneth became the *'Bride of God'* a wife to the virgin Joseph. The father of Aseneth was called Pentephres, he was a priest of the Egyptian gods. The love of God is amazing and hard to fathom. Aseneth did not like men and did not worship the living God; her dress code was that which made her distinct as a worshipper of the Egyptian gods. All these disqualified her from being a wife to Joseph. From the time of his youth Joseph was taught by his father Jacob never to marry gentiles (Jub. 40:5-8), but we realise the love and power of our God (Florenza, 1995). In preparation for her marriage to Joseph, Aseneth had an encounter with God, where she then repented and asked for God's forgiveness of her sin. They then got married and Aseneth gave birth to two boys; Manasseh and Ephraim (Genesis 41:50-51).

The devil is angry about your invitation

At the beginning of this book, we talked about how Lucifer was God's great angel worshipper: 'light-bearer.' Satan is very angry, because he will spend his eternal life tortured and tormented in hell. The devil knows the beauty, joy and peace in heaven. His goal is to steal, kill and destroy humanity (John 10:10). One of the strategies he used to accomplish this goal is to blind humanity so that they ignore God's invitation, making various excuses for not accepting God's love. The devil influences the will of humanity so that they rebel against God, for example as seen in the parable of the wedding feast, where landlords killed God's servants. The prophets, priests, ministers and preachers are all God's servants assigned to announce that humanity is invited to the royal wedding feast. Some of the servants of God were killed by the Pharisees, scribes and chief priests. For example, John the Baptist was beheaded by King Herod, with the influence of his wife

(Matthew 14:1-2); Stephen was stoned to death by the Israelites, because he reminded them that they resisted the Holy Spirit and persecuted the prophets of God, just like their forefathers (Acts 7:51-60). Many servants of God are being killed even up to this day.

The devil influences humanity to belittle the Word of God. This is a similar strategy to the one he used in the Garden of Eden: *"Did God really say you must not eat the fruit from any of the trees in the garden?"* (Genesis 3:1). It is apparent that the devil continues to influence humanity to belittle the Word of God. At times he encourages humanity to rationalise and justify why they much decline the love of God and His invitation to the royal wedding. For example, I have heard several people justifying why God will not allow people to go to hell, arguing: *"how can God create us and then let us die in hell?"*. You might have heard similar argument in the past, please write them below. You may also write similar examples from the Bible.

Seeing that the invited guests declined attending the wedding feast, God then extended his invitation to everyone. He informed the servants to go to the streets corners and invite anyone and everyone; the good and the bad. Soon the banquet hall was full. The servants' call and invitation to the wedding feast represent the gospel offer given to humanity. This is very profound, signifying the fact that God's love has been extended to humanity in the world: these are His guests; Jew and gentiles, good and bad (Matthew 28:9; Mark 13:10; Mark 16:15; Romans 1:16; Revelation 14:6). The blood of Jesus Christ washes and cleanses all sins; it makes good the bad. This is true salvation from sin.

The Royal Wedding garment

I have been fortunate to watch three royal weddings in the United Kingdom. One of the outstanding features I have observed is the dress code for all invited guests, especially the members of the royal family. All guests (men and women) were beautifully and smartly dressed and they seem to follow the queen and her husband, in their dress code. In the same way, those who accept the invitation to the royal heavenly wedding feast must accept and wear a unique and specific type of attire. This dress code sets the bride apart for God alone; it separates her from those who decline the invitation. It is a dress of righteousness.

One of the guests chose not to wear the allocated wedding dress. This guest represents hypocrites who are in the church, but are not for the church. This rebellious guest represents those who are in the church, they may participant in various religious activities, but do not produce the fruits of the Holy Spirit; they do not have attributes which show that they are set apart for God. This means that those who accept Jesus as their Lord and Saviour must (with the help of the Holy Spirit) live a righteous life; display or demonstrate the fruits of the Spirit (Galatians 5:22,23) without which one will be thrown into the lake of fire (Hebrews 12:14).

The following verses further deliberate on the description of the wedding garment. *"Everything I did was honest. Righteousness covered me like a robe, and I wore justice like a turban"* (Job 29:14).

"Because we belong to the day, we must live decent lives for all to see. Don't participate in the darkness of wild parties and drunkenness, or in sexual promiscuity and immoral living, or in quarrelling and jealousy. Instead, clothe yourself with the presence of the Lord Jesus Christ. And don't let yourself think about ways to indulge your evil desires" Romans 13:13-14.

"For all of you who were baptized into Christ have clothed yourselves with Christ" (Galatians 3:27).

"Let us rejoice and be glad and give the glory to Him, for the marriage of the Lamb has come and His bride has made herself ready." It was given to her to clothe herself in fine linen, bright and clean; for the fine linen is the righteous acts of the saints (Revelation 19:7-8).

"Blessed are those who wash their robes. They will be permitted to enter through the gates of the city and eat the fruit from the tree of life (Revelation 22:14).

Based on these verses, please make notes on your understanding of the description of the wedding garment.

The wedding hall was completely packed with guests, the majority had been prepared by accepting and wearing the wedding garment. No comment was made about the one guest who did not wear the wedding dress, until the king came into the gathering to welcome his guests. This means that judgement belongs to God alone. As followers of Christ no one can judge the other regarding their readiness or fitness to partake in the royal wedding feast. Additionally, while humanity can manage to hide iniquities from each other, no one can hide them from God, because he knows and searches all the hearts of humanity *"I am watching them closely, and I see every sin. They cannot hope to hide from me"* (Jeremiah 16:17). Please read Psalms 33:13.

I learnt about the importance of being honest at all times the hard way. One day I was rushing to work, because I had left home late. As I was passing through town I quickly jumped through the red light and proceeded with my journey. Just before turning to the street that led to my place of work, I was stopped by a man driving a 'normal' car. A police officer quickly came to me and introduced himself; as he put on his police coat, he showed me his identity badge. He then informed me that he had been following me since I had driven through a red traffic light in town, ten minutes ago. I had to pay the consequences of being dishonest (jumping through a red traffic light). This taught me a big lesson, that the best thing to do in life is to ensure that whatever I do in secret I can also confidently do in public, because someone even greater that a police officer is always watching my actions and I will soon give an account of everything I have done while in this world (Romans 14:11-13; 2 Corinthians 5:10).

Please read the previous verses in Romans and 2 Corinthians. Have a moment of silence (you can close your eyes if you want) with the help of the Holy Spirit think about those things which might not be acceptable and/or could result in one being disqualified from participating in the royal wedding feast.

Please take a moment of silence as you reflect on the characters in the parable of the wedding feast. Which of the characters in this parable do you represent and why? Are you happy about being this character? Please write your answers below.

Following the above reflection, please spend some time in prayer, talking to God to help you either remain dressed in the God given garment or ask Him to forgive you for not accepting his garment; accept it and ask Him to help you keep it clean, ready for his return: *"Yet there are some in the church in Sardis who have not soiled their clothes with evil. They will walk with me in white, for they are worthy"* Revelation 3:4.

Then one of the twenty-four elders asked me, "who are these who are clothed in white? Where did they come from? And I said to him, "Sir, you are the one who knows." Then he said to me "These are the ones who died in the great tribulation. They have washed their robes in the blood of the Lamb and made them white" Revelation 7:13-14.

The Unknown Day

The aim of this book is to announce the greatest invitation to humanity; to the royal wedding feast; where humanity is given the top position: she is the bride. Those who choose to accept the invitation must also accept and put on the wedding garment: by living a life separated for God. When He departed to heaven, Jesus informed His disciples that He was going to return to earth to take His bride/church to spend eternity with Him in heaven. Even though He informed us about signs for his return, Jesus does not know the specific date, day and time of His return; this is only known by God the Father (Matthew 24:36). As a result, Jesus emphasised that humanity MUST be ready (Matthew 24:44). Jesus illustrated this by narrating another parable: The parable of the ten virgins (Matthew 25:1-13).

Before we discuss the parable of the ten bridesmaids we will look at the indicators of His return according to what He said in Matthew 24. Please read this chapter and make notes about what Jesus said on the following:

The end of the world in Matthew 24:1-22.

False messiahs Matthew 24:22-28.

The return of the Son of Man Matthew 24:29-36.

His sudden return: Matthew 24:37-41.

How to be ready for his return Matthew 24:42-50.

From your reading above please make notes on how you see some of the above predictions being realised or fulfilled in this contemporary world.

Matthew 25:1-13: The Parable of the Ten Virgins

Humanity has a very important decision to make while living in this world. They must first decide about their eternal destination of their soul/spirit: heaven or hell. After making this decision (Heaven, hopefully) they must do two things: **Be alert and ready.** This is a must to all who are going to attend the royal wedding feast. To make His point clearer, Jesus told his disciples about the parable of the ten virgins or bridesmaids. Please read Matthew 25:1-13 then make notes on the following:

Main points

Understood meaning

Importance of this parable

Be ready in the delay

The ten virgins/bridesmaids represent those who have chosen to accept Jesus as their Lord and Saviour. They are also known as: the body of Christ, the church, the elect, the bride. The virgins were waiting to escort the bridegroom (Jesus Christ our Lord) in a torch-light procession as He brought His bride home. Each of the virgins had their torches. These torches used oil-soaked rags to keep them burning and provide light; as such they needed a continuous supply of oil to keep burning, without which they would be extinguished.

Jesus is teaching his disciples about the importance of being ready for His second return to earth, to take His bride to heaven. Five of the bridesmaids were ready and the others were not. For whatever reason, the groom was delayed, such that all the bridesmaids slumbered and fell asleep. Similar to the ten bridesmaids, the bride of Jesus Christ may be tempted to relax and start living a careless life, forgetting that they are waiting for the return of the groom (Jesus). Even though the five wise bridesmaids had their lamps lit throughout the night, they failed to be awake and watch for the coming of the groom; all the virgins fell asleep. This means that Christians must watch out for slumber and gradual spiritual decay. For example, this might be a result of engaging or not engaging in activities which were once considered as unacceptable by the Lord; or eliminating those activities which are of importance to enhance spiritual growth and readiness for the return of the groom.

Please think about some of the things you think are being omitted by the church, which predisposes her to being locked outside on the return of the groom. Also identity activities which are incorporated into the bride, yet are likely to delay the bride from entering the royal wedding feast.

Added by Bride = Absent at the Feast	Omitted by Bride = Absent at the Feast
Anger and bitterness	Prayer and fasting

Preparations guarantees entry to the feast

A shout was heard at midnight; the groom was coming, that it was time to go out and meet him. The virgins were then expected to light their lamps. The lamps of five virgins had sustained light, because they had prepared for the event by bringing extra oil. These were the wise virgins. On the other hand, the other five virgins (foolish) only realised, at the arrival of the groom, that they did not have enough oil. They started panicking asking that the wise virgins share their oil with them; unfortunately, this was not possible. The wise virgins suggested that the foolish virgins go to the shops to buy some oil; they took the advice and went away. Meanwhile, the groom arrived at the wedding feast entered and locked the door. On their return, the foolish virgins knocked and pleaded that the groom should open the door for them, but the groom replied: *"Believe me, I do not know you."* This statement is similar to a previous one, stated by Jesus, as discussed in Lesson 8. Please reflect back and make notes on what you think are the similarities and or differences within these texts.

In this parable Jesus stated that the date and time of His second return is not known by anyone even Himself; His return to collect His bride will be sudden and will take place at a time no-one anticipates. Please enumerate specific things done by the two sets of virgins which separated them from each other and the consequences of their activities: the wise from the foolish.

What the foolish virgins did differently from the wise.

Consequences

What the wise virgins did differently from the foolish.

Consequences

Please take some time and think about some of the characteristics/activities of the church today, then indicate how they fit in either of the two sets of virgins (foolish and wise). That is, as a bride of Christ how can one recognise their readiness or alertness for the return of the Lord Jesus Christ, our bridegroom.

The Five Foolish Virgins Today	The Five Wise Virgins Today

At the beginning of this lesson, we talked about the parable of the wedding feast. We discussed about the importance of accepting and wearing the wedding garment, specifically designed for the royal wedding ceremony. The best decision for any human being is to accept the love of God by receiving Jesus Christ into their life. Their names are then written in the royal book of Life and they are given a new garment. It is the responsibility of the owner of the dress to make sure that the garment is not only put on, but that it is kept clean at all times. This is one of the indicators of being ready for the return of the groom. There are a number of ways to ensure being ready and alert for Jesus' return. Please read the verses below and make notes on how the bride can ensure that their garments are ready for the royal wedding celebration.

1. Be alert and ready by being sober minded and through prayer: 1 Peter 4:7; Matthew 26:41; Luke 22:46.

2. Alert and ready by living today as if He is coming back today: Luke 19:11-27.

3. Alert and ready by asking the Holy Spirit to help the bride discern various spirits so that we are not deceived: 2 Thessalonians 2:1-3.

4. Alert and ready by staying away from sin and cleansing their garment in the blood of the lamb Revelation 7:14.

5. Alert and ready by reading the Word of God (the Bible), it helps the bride to keep the garment clean by staying away from sin: Psalms 119:11.

6. Alert and ready because no one knows the day of His return: Mark 13:32-33.

7. Alert and ready by being confident and hoping in the truthfulness of His Word: Titus 2:11-13.

8. Alert and ready by reminding and encouraging each other about the return of the bridegroom: 1 Thessalonians 4:16-18; 5:2, 3 &11.

9. Alert and ready by telling and leading others to Christ: Matthew 28:19; Mark 13:10.

10. Alert and ready by wearing the whole armour of God, our enemy the devil prowls around looking for someone to devour: 1 Thessalonians 5:6; 1 Peter 5:8; Ephesian 6:10-20.

READY, ALERT and APPROPRIATELY DRESSED: ALWAYS

Jesus talked about the need and importance of being ready and alert for His return, at all times; this is very significant if we are to attend His wedding feast. Humanity must be ready for His return, because it will be unannounced and will happen in a twinkle of an eye (suddenly). There will be no opportunity to amend or change anything which should have been dealt with before. Similar to the situation with the five foolish virgins, there was no time to purchase the extra oil and as a result they were denied entrance on their return. The door was shut. Any lack of God's standard of righteous living will result in that individual being left behind and entry into the wedding feast will be permanently denied. Jesus will say: *"Believe me, I do not know you."* This means that the relationship between humanity and Jesus MUST start today, while we are still living on this earth.

Humanity must then live a life of being separated from the things of this world: righteous living. This will guarantee entry into Jesus' wedding feast. As already discussed in previous lessons; the starting point of the journey to the royal wedding ceremony is repentance. The individual must acknowledge and confess sin with their mouth, then accept Jesus into their life. This is then followed by living a righteous life; through the help of the Holy Spirit. Below is a glimpse illustration of the tables which has been prepared for the royal wedding feast. It is going to be an event never to be missed. May our good Father, Son and the Holy Spirt open the eyes of humanity to realise that God has great, good things in store for humanity; the key is accepting His love and living a life set apart for Him, until He takes us to the prepared royal feast. As you reflect and think about the good things instore for the bride in heaven, please read Isaiah 64:4 and reflect on 1 Corinthians 2:9:

"Eye has not seen, nor ear heard, Nor have entered into the heart of man The things which God has prepared for those who love Him."

Illustrates The Royal Wedding Tablet

After making this decision the devil becomes angry and furious at humanity, for denouncing him and escaping eternal separation from God. This is the beginning of a spiritual warfare; where the devil uses various tactics to interrupt the smooth relationship of the Christian with God. In the next lesson we will explore the various strategies used by the devil to prevent humanity from entering the wedding feast and how to overcome them. Christians must know about their enemy and must be confident in the fight, because the war has already been won by our Lord Jesus Christ; through His death on the cross and His resurrection. To crown it all, Jesus is sat at the right hand of God, praying and interceding that humanity conquers (as Jesus did) and enter their celebration at the wedding feast and their rest in heaven. Please read the following verses and make notes on your understanding on why Christians must be confident about facing their enemy, the devil.

Hebrew 7:25

Romans 8:34

Romans 8:37

After He is accepted into the heart of humanity, Jesus makes a home in the lives of the individual, so that He walks with them, talks, sleeps and does everything with them (Revelation 3:20). This is the greatest gift to humanity, no wonder Jesus is Emmanuel, God with us (Isaiah 7:14; Matthew1:22-23). Paul asked the Church: *"Do you not know that you are the temple of God and that the Spirit of God dwells in you"* 1 Corinthians 3:16. Christians have got the power of God within them and this is what makes them more than conquerors as they face all the challenges in this journey of life (Romans 8:31-39).

As a Christian it is easy to be overwhelmed by challenges and difficult situations faced along the journey of life, so that you either attempt to fight with your own strength or run away from facing the enemy. Even though the disciples of Jesus had been with Him for some time, they did not comprehend who He is, His power and dominion over everything. They were initially terrified when hit by the storm at sea, until they remembered to wake Him up, to ask for help. Jesus rebuked the storm and it quickly calmed down. The disciples asked *"Who can this be, that even the wind and the sea obey Him!"* Mark 4:35-41. The same Jesus who calmed the storm is the one who lives in the heart and lives of all those who accept Him. Humanity and Christians can call upon Him at any time, for He is always ready to help (Psalms 50:15; Joel 2:42; Acts 2:21; Romans 10:13).

Please spare a moment and think about challenges you might be going through today, those situations which appear too difficult to solve. Please list them below so that you can hand them over to Jesus, because He has a solution and is ready to help you, as we have already seen in the previous verses.

Please spend some time in prayer, handing over the list above to Jesus for He is going to help you solve the problems and you will soon marvel and testify about his miraculous interventions. By putting on the whole armour of God you are able to overcome the temptations of the devil. The next lesson discusses how the bride of Christ overcome challenges they face as they travel this world. Using this armour is important to ensure arrival to the royal wedding feast.

Identity Determines Your Final Destiny

Before we explore the spiritual attire of the bride of Jesus Christ (the whole armour of God) we will briefly discuss the importance of the identity of humanity as defined by God, their creator.

Identity is defined as *"Who you are, the way you think about yourself...... the characteristics that define you"* (https://www.yourdictionary.com/identity).The best way to define yourself is through your creator.

Our true identity is only found in Jesus Christ; the Saviour of the world. We have already seen in the previous lessons that humanity was created by God in His image, they are alive because of the spirit breathed by God. We also talked about Mercedes Benz and the importance of consulting the manufacturer for missing parts and maintained. Likewise, in order to be able to authentically define who you are it is important to refer to your creator, God. If you let God tell you who you are, you have endless confidence in who you are and will never let others put you down. Your self-esteem is enhanced because you know that you are fearfully and wonderfully made, that you are the apple of God's eye.

A clearly defined identify influences you in the choices and decisions you make in daily life, in fulfilling your God given purpose. Because he knew his identity, Daniel purposed not to defile himself with the king's delicacies (Daniel 1:8), in the end, Daniel received the favour of God and he was the wisest of the all, even ten times better than all the magicians and astrologers of his time (Daniel 1:20).

A well-defined identity influences your choice to accept the invitation to the royal wedding feast; to accept and wear the royal wedding gown and to ensure that it is kept clean at all times, until the return of Jesus Christ. The prodigal son had lost his identity when he decided to eat with the pigs: he identified himself as a pig. He had forgotten who he was: that he was from a rich family, where his father's servants had a lot of food to eat (Luke 15:11-32). It was only when *"he came to himself"* (Luke 15:17); that he remembered who he was; this led to a clearly defined identity and his thought process, journey, direction, destination changed. The prodigal son went back to his roots and was gladly welcomed by his father.

The parable of the prodigal son is a clear demonstration of the fact that humanity's identity can be swallowed by various life challenges. During these times it is likely that humanity focuses on the challenges and attempt to resolve the problems by themselves. We realise in the parable of the prodigal son that the young man was desperate for money and he was hungry. This problem was easily solved when he came back to himself: when he remembered his identity. On his arrival at home there was so much celebration and a lot of food to eat, his very need. As such, it is apparent that: knowing your identify in Christ is a solution to overcome the challenges we face. Please take a moment to reflect on some of the day-to-day challenges which you think takes away the identity of humanity in Christ. Kindly make a list of these below:

Before the actual discussion about the royal wedding feast, please take some time to find verses from the Bible which describe your identify in Christ. On the next page there is a list of some of the statements which define your identity. You can affirm these attributes as you do the Bible search.

God Says I Am	Evidence: Bibles Verses
His image	
Productive and fruitful	
Fearfully and wonderfully made	
The apple of His eye	

The head and not the tail	
Surrounded by His angels	
More than a conqueror	
Saved by grace	
Created to excel	
Safe from all the weapons of my enemies	
Loved unconditionally	
Forgiven from all my sins	
Will be like Him when He returns	
His child	
Chosen by Him	
Free to confidently talk to Him at anytime	
Given all power above all evil	
Free to ask Him for anything	
Made righteous through Jesus Christ	
The temple where He lives	
His intimate friend	
Destined for eternal fellowship with Him	
Anointed	

Created to fulfil His unique purpose	
Free from the bondage of sin	
Complete in Him	
Seated with Christ in the heavenly realm	
The heavenly heir	
A citizen of heaven	
Able to do all things through Christ	
Create to overcome the world	
Have power to create with my tongue	
Living out of darkens into His light	
The salt of the earth	
An ambassador for Christ	
Created for good works	
Blessed and highly favoured	
The light of the world	
Who God says I am	

LESSON 11
Over-comers by Design

Introduction

Humanity is God's creation, but they have an enemy, Lucifer, Satan, the devil. At the beginning of our lessons we learnt how Lucifer was cast out of heaven, because he disobeyed God and fell into sin; he now awaits his eternal torture and torment in hell. We also discussed that the mission of the devil is to recruit as many people as possible to be destroyed along with him in hell. Satan is constantly fighting humanity: killing, stealing and destroying them and all that belongs to them. After an individual accepts Jesus Christ as their Lord and Saviour the devil does not rest, but his fighting mission against humanity intensifies. His goal is to influence them to give up before their arrival to the royal wedding feast, or if they enter, he wants them to be disqualified, because of the lack of righteousness in their lives. The devil wants humanity to be eternally separated from God, in hell where he is destined. We are ever so grateful to the Holy Spirit who guides and protects humanity as they travel this Christian walk. Additionally, Jesus is now seated at the right hand of God, interceding that all the children of God win the victory and enter their rest in heaven. So, we can confidently say: *"if God is for us, who can be against us?"* Romans 8:31. In this chapter we are going to discuss one of God's given strategy for Christians to fight the devil; using the armour of God.

This is a battlefield not a playground

Finally, my brethren, be strong in the Lord and in the power of His might. Put on the whole armour of God, that you may be able to stand against the wiles of the devil. For we do not wrestle against flesh and blood, but against principalities, against powers, against spiritual hosts of wickedness in the heavenly places. Therefore, take up the whole armour of God, that you may be able to withstand in the evil day, and having done all, to stand. Stand therefore, having girded your waist with truth, having put on the breastplate of righteousness, and having shod your feet with the preparation of the gospel of peace; above all, taking the shield of faith with which you will be able to quench all the fiery darts of the wicked one. And take the helmet of salvation, and the sword of the Spirit, which is the Word of God; praying always with all prayer and supplication in the Spirit, being watchful to this end with all perseverance and supplication for all the saints-

Ephesians 6:10-18

Humanity is in this world to fight; until they relocate to their spiritual destination. The above verse is the core of this lesson; the God given strategy to His children to overcome the war against the devil. In the book of Revelation chapters 12 to 16 we learn about the war waged by the devil, against God and His children. The devil is an enemy to humanity, because they are God's creation, created in his image. Humans are loved and treasured by God, He desires and enjoys endless fellowship with them. God has created heaven for all who choose and accept His love. While humanity has not been to heaven, the devil lived there and is fully aware of the joy and treasures which awaits all those who choose heaven as their eternal destination.

The devil has limited powers. Unlike God who is all knowing, all powerful and present everywhere all over heaven and earth at the same time (omniscient; omnipotent; omnipresent), Satan has none of these attributes. Satan uses the fallen angels to fight humanity and to rule this world. These are also referred to as *'principalities, powers, rulers, spiritual wickedness in high places'* (Ephesian 6:12). This means that we are not fighting against humanity, but against the invisible world: spiritual wickedness in high places. Therefore, instead of fighting humans we must confront and fight the devil who controls humanity. The devil is always walking around the earth, influencing humanity to

164

do evil, so that they are kept separated from God their creator; while they live on earth and though eternity (2 Peter 2:4; Jude 1:6, Revelation 12:9). The devil uses humanity as hosts, as we have already discussed in Lesson 5.

All in all, Satan does not want humanity to participate in the wedding ceremony of our Lord Jesus Christ. For those who have accepted the invitation the devil continuously fights them, so that they either enter the ceremony not wearing the wedding garment, or their garments are spoiled or defiled. This means that the devil constantly attempts to influence Christians not to live a righteous life so that they will be disqualified entry to eternal life. This earth is a battlefield. Kindly read the following verses and make notes on the insight you receive from the texts, regarding the 'war'.

1 Timothy 6:12

Romans 8: 37

Revelation 21:7

The goal of the devil is to kill, steal and destroy (John 10:10). Ephesians 2:1-2 states: *"Once you were dead because of your disobedience and your many sins. You used to live in sin, just like the rest of the world, obeying the devil-the commander of the powers in the unseen world. He is the spirit at work in the hearts of those who refuse to obey God."* Although he presents as a good person: angel of light (2 Corinthians 4:11) and as a wolf in a sheep's skin (Matthew 7:15), Satan is very evil, he has no mercy and no interest in humanity.

As we have already seen at the beginning of our lessons, the devil influences humanity to become his hosts to target other human beings; whether they have accepted Jesus as Lord and Saviour or not. Satan influences humanity's power of the will, so that they make wrong choices, ones which will continuously separate them from having a good relationship with God. He targets all the aspects of humanity (body, soul, spirit). Ephesians 2:1-2 states: *"Once you were dead because of your disobedience and your many sins. You used to live in sin, just like the rest of the world, obeying the devil-the commander of the powers in the unseen world. He is the spirit at work in the hearts of those who refuse to obey God."*

The devil blinds humanity from seeing and accepting the love of God and he persuades Christians to backslide, going back to sin. It is very important to know the plans and tactics of our enemy so that we can be able fight victoriously, using the correct equipment. Ignoring the devices of the devil can cost humanity their eternal life, hence, it is important that we know about him and his strategies (2 Corinthian 2:11). ***"Unless we know who the enemy is, where he is and what he can do, we have a difficult time defeating him."*** *(Wiersbe Warren, David Cook, 2007, p622)*. The writing of Paul in Ephesians 6:10-12 clearly indicates that the enemy to the bride of Jesus is **strong**. One vivid example of the manifestation of his power is in the life of Job; where he killed his children, destroyed his home, wealth, body and friends (Job 1-3). Our enemy is also cunning and crafty. This is one of the reasons Paul urges the bride to put on the whole armour of God; so that they can be able to *'stand against the wiles'* of the devil.

The devil's aim is to alienate humanity from God by influencing and causing them to rebel and disobey God. He causes humanity to be corrupt in their thinking and makes them to be ignorant about the truth of God, as such they will produce evil acts, because of their evil thoughts. The devil also influences the division amongst humanity as a result of evil attitudes; like greed, anger and bitterness. We shall look at some of the devil's strategies to prevent humanity from having a continuous smooth relationship with God. Please read the following verses then elaborate on the strategies used by the devil to fight humanity. Mention how he has used or may use each of the strategies in your life.

Deceit: Matthew 7:15; 2 Corinthians 11:14; Revelation 12:8

Life examples

Spiritual blindness: 2 Corinthians 4: 3-4

Life examples

An Accuser: Job 1:9-10; Revelation 12:10

Life examples

Destroys: John 10:10

Example in your life

Liars: John 8:44

Life examples

The devil is also referred to as the father to all liars John 8:44. He lies about everything and there is no truth that comes from his mouth. Those who follow the devil also have no truth in them, they always lie. Some of the lies from the devil and his angels are listed below. Please read the verse and make notes about the truths from the Word of God, refuting the lies of the devil.

1. That **God is not interested in you:** because of the many sins you have done. Luke 5:31-32

2. That you can **never find true love and happiness** in this world. This is not true because of the words of Jesus in John 24:27.

3. **God does not care about how we behave, because he loves you.** This is not true because of what the word of God says in Romans 12:1-2; 1 Peter 1:15-16.

4. **Confessing your sins is not good, because it hurts other people.** This is not true, it perpetrates the spirit of deceit, similar to what King Saul did. Unfortunately listening to this lie gives birth to other liars and hinders the success and progress of humanity. God wants us to confess our sins, because this is what restores our relationship with him. Proverbs 28:13; 1 John 1: 9-10.

5. **You do not need the teachings of the church because they are outdated.** Most of the time the devil tells people that the preachers want to collect money from the members, so it is better not to attend church. But fellowship is very important amongst Christians; Act 2:42-47; Hebrews 10:25.

6. **You cannot make it to heaven and you are trying but are failing**. Ephesians 2:8-9; Galatians 3:10-12

More Than Conquerors

At the end of his letter to the brethren at Ephesus, Paul urged them to be strong in the Lord and in the power of His might. The strategy to do this is by putting on the WHOLE armour of God. Christians destined to heaven must choose to wear the complete armour, if they are to win the battle against the devil. From the time they were created, humanity was given an assignment or command to subdue/overcome the world, as we have already seen in Lesson 1 (Genesis 1:28). This was stated by God and in His faithfulness, God gave humanity the strategies, power and ability to overcome evil. For this very reason John stated that *"For whatever is born of God overcomes the world: and this is the victory that overcomes the world, even our faith"* 1 John 5:4. We give God the glory because within the book of Revelation John also explained that humanity overcomes the war waged by the devil *"by the blood of the lamp and by the word of their testimony"* Revelation 12:11.

The Whole Armour of God

The devil wages war against the bride of Jesus Christ from the following sources: the **world**, the **flesh** and the **devil** himself (Ephesians 2:1-3). The world is defined as the society in the absence of God. Its aims and objectives are contrary to those of the bride of Christ. The systems of the world focus on fulfilling all the physical things or those which are visible, these are: the lust of the flesh, the lust of the eyes and the pride of life (1 John 2:15-17). The seed of sin which entered humanity in the Garden of Eden is referred to as the flesh. The flesh is always in conflict with the spirit. Please think about some examples of how the devil fights the bride in each of the following areas:

The world

The flesh

The devil

The good news is that all three sources of war against the bride were defeated by the death and resurrection of our Lord Jesus Christ.

According to John 16:33 and Galatians 6:14 Jesus conquered the **world;** Ephesians 1:19-23 reveals that **Satan** was defeated by our Lord Jesus Christ. The **flesh** was also defeated according to Romans 6:1-6 and Galatians 2:20. Therefore, this means that Christians do not fight for victory, but they are fighting from victory, because Jesus has already won the battle. Please reflect on the above paragraph, you may read the above verses and make notes on your thoughts and understanding of Jesus' victory over the war against the people of God.

The devil is very clever and highly knowledgeable. He is also very angry and jealous that he is no longer allowed in heaven, but awaits hell where he will be eternally tortured and tormented (Revelation 12:12). This makes it paramount for all Christians to put on the FULL armour of God, if they are to participate at the royal wedding ceremony. 'Putting' on the armour means that the act is deliberate, it must be done intentionally. To the church of Corinth Paul wrote: *"We are human, but we don't wage war as humans do. We use God's mighty weapons, not worldly weapons, to knock down the strongholds of arguments. We destroy every proud obstacle that keeps people from knowing God. We capture their rebellious thoughts and teach them to obey Christ"* 2 Corinthians 10: 3-5.

The Holy Spirit lives in Christians, those who receive Him (John 14:17). He helps Christians to fight a good fight of faith. Please read the following verses then enumerate how the Holy Spirit helps the bride of Christ to fight the battle to the royal wedding ceremony.

John 14:26

John 15:26

John 16:8-13

John 16: 14-15

The church is instructed to 'stand strong,' like a solider ready for war. Christians must stand their ground; they are to stand firm. Their source of strength is only found in the Lord Jesus. Standing makes it necessary for the bride to be fully alert and ready, as they put on the whole armour of God. On their own the church cannot stand strong, but their strength is only found in the mighty power of God through the Holy Spirit. Therefore, putting the whole armour of God is an essential entity for a victorious Christian. This is important because their enemy the devil is crafty and cunning. The intelligence of humanity cannot defend them from the attacks of the devil.

The posture of being stood up reminds us of the parable of the ten virgins; where Jesus teaches His bride that they must be alert and ready, not only to fight the devil, but must be ready and alert for His return to earth. This means that as soldiers of Christ, Christians must be awake at all times and not fall asleep. The spiritual armour of God must be worn by the bride of our Lord Jesus Christ, at all times. It is not a physical attire; but a figurative armour which was initially spoken about by the prophet Isaiah: *"For He put on righteousness as a breastplate, And a helmet of salvation on His head; He put on the garments of vengeance for clothing, And was clad with zeal as a cloak"* Isaiah 59:17. Yet the evidence of putting it on is revealed in all aspects of the human life. Below is a picture to show how a Christian puts on the armour of God, from head to toe. We will discuss the individual items of the armour next.

Helmet of Salvation

Breastplate of Righteousness

Sheild of Faith

Belt of Truth

Sword of The Spirit

Spread the Gospel of Peace

The Whole Armour of God

1. The Belt/Girdle of Truth

"Stand therefore, having fastened on the belt of truth......"

Ephesians 6:14

Jesus told his disciples the truth: *"I am the way, the truth and the life. No one comes to the father except through me."* (John 4:6). One of the devil's attributes is that he is a liar and the father of lies (John 8:44). The devil used lies to convince Adam and Eve to fall into sin. Firstly, putting on the belt of truth liberates humanity from the lies and deceit of the devil. There is no truth in everything he says. It is amazing to note that the first item listed by Paul when putting on the armour is the belt of truth. Knowing the truth brings freedom and liberty to humanity and the truth is knowing the Word of God: Jesus our Lord. This was stated by Jesus in John 8:31-32 *"If you abide in my word, you are my disciples indeed. And you shall know the truth, and the truth shall make you free."*

The Pharisees did not understand what Jesus meant when he said they would be free, because they believed that they were free, since they belong to Abraham. Jesus stated: *"......Most assuredly, I say to you, whoever commits sin is a slave of sin. And a slave does not abide in the house forever, but a son abides forever. Therefore, if the Son sets you free, you shall be free indeed."* John 8:34-36. This means that knowing the truth leads to repentance and freedom from sin. This freedom reveals the identity of humanity, in Christ. Once they know their identity, humanity is able to pursue and live their God given purpose: *"Then God blessed them, and God said to them, be fruitful and multiply: fill the earth and subdue it......"* Genesis 1:28.

Please take a moment to think about some of the false labels which you might have been given by the devil, perhaps some he has given you as a result of difficulties, failures and challenges you have gone through. It might have been through hearing his voice or even through other people giving you labels or calling you names. Please write them below.

Please take some time to report the above lies to the Lord and ask for forgiveness for accepting the false labels from the devil. Ask the Holy Spirit to give you strength to resist the lies from the devil as you put on your belt of truth. Amen!

The second benefit of putting on the belt of truth is that once the individual has been set free from sin the belt of truth continues to liberate them from the ongoing lies of the devil. They are able to live a life of integrity and honesty, with a clear conscience. As a result, such an individual faces Satan without fear. The belt of truth is important, because it holds the sword in place. This means that if we live a truthful life, we can use the Word of truth (the sword of the Spirit) to defeat the devil. It is important to guard against the lies of the devil, because if permitted to enter the life of a Christian, one lie gives birth to another lies until the devil finds a place of habitation. We have already discussed the story of David in the previous lessons, how he lied about his sin with the wife of Uriah. Subsequently, his lies resulted in the murder of Uriah.

Take a moment and think about your belt of truth. Mull over the following: Do you have it on you? Mention some examples or how you used or did not use the belt of truth. What are your plans about the importance of this item of the armour of God?

2. Breastplate of righteousness

"......and having put on the breastplate of righteousness" Ephesians 6:14

This is a metal body covering which protects the Christian at the front and back of the upper body, from the neck to the waist. It symbolises the righteousness of the warriors of Christ. Righteousness means complete and perfect obedience to God's standard of living; this is how the bride of Christ is expected to live. Also, a Christian living without righteousness is exposed to attacks and defeats of the devil. Holiness is God's standard of living for all those who are to participate at the royal wedding feast. This is revealed by accepting and wearing the wedding garment.

Please read the following verses: *"Let us be glad and rejoice and give Him glory, for the marriage of the Lamb has come, and His wife has made herself ready.' And to her it was granted to be arrayed in fine linen, clean and bright, for the fine linen is the righteous acts of the saints."* Revelation 19:7-8. Make notes on your insight on the following:

The wedding garment

Definition of righteousness

It is the responsibility of the bride to make sure that the garment is kept clean, at all times (Hebrew 12:14). In the parable of the wedding feast Jesus talked about one of the guests who was disqualified from the wedding ceremony, because they were not wearing the wedding garment. The wedding garment represents righteousness; that is God's standard of living. His standard is that of being separated for Him: living a holy life.

Those who choose to accept the love of Jesus Christ are also expected to live and adhere to righteous living and reflect their separateness for

God in their daily living. At the beginning of this book we realised that God used the principle of separation during creation. For example, God separated light from darkness; day from night; land from water, to name a few. He also commanded the Israelites to be set apart or be separated for Him alone: being holy. The breast plate of righteousness indicates that Christians must live a life completely set apart for God; being righteous in Christ (2 Corinthians 5:21) and live a righteous life in Christ (Ephesians 4:24). This piece of armour protects the Christian from the accusations made by the devil, so that when he makes an accusation the righteousness of Christ assures the Christian of their salvation and victory over sin.

Please read the following scriptures and make notes about the importance of practising righteousness:

1 John 2:29

2 Timothy 2:2

Job and Joseph are some examples of individuals who wore their breastplate of righteousness, throughout good and difficult times. Their breastplate of righteousness protected them from the accusations brought by the devil. Their focus was to maintain a good standing with God. The word of God is fundamental in helping Christians live a righteous life: *"All scripture is given by inspiration of God, and is profitable for doctrine, for reproof, for correction, for instruction in righteousness."* 2 Timothy 3:16. It is significant to note that the description of this metaphor (breastplate) has different representation. In the book of 1 Thessalonians 5:8 the breastplate represents faith and love yet, in the book of Ephesians it represents righteousness. Nevertheless, all three explanations are important in protecting Christians. Please read the following verses and make notes on how Christians can conquer the devil when they put on the breastplate of

177

faith and love. Love conquers everything and enhances peace and harmony among the people of God.

Faith: Matthew 17:20

Love: 1 Peter 4:8

3. Shoes: Good News Gospel of Peace

"For shoes, put on the peace that comes from the Good News so that you will be fully prepared......" Ephesians 6:15.

The bride of Jesus Christ received and accepted the gospel of peace brought to humanity through the cross of Jesus Christ. This gospel promotes reconciliation, inner peace or a peaceful conscience and peace among the saints. One of the blessings received by humanity when they reconcile with God is unspeakable peace (Roman 5:1). In the previous lessons we discussed about the fact that this blessing is not available for sale anywhere around the world, and that it cannot be manufactured anywhere. This peace gives Christians the confidence to fight against their enemy through the knowledge that *"......greater is he who is in them that he that is in the world"* 1 John 4:4 and that they are *"more than conquerors through Jesus Christ our Lord"* Roman 8:37.

God commands humanity to be at peace and harmony with each other (James 4:1-7) and this is one strategy which helps the bride to defeat the devil. In previous lessons we also discussed about how anger and bitterness could prevent humanity from being accepted into the royal wedding ceremony. Along with living a holy life, God commands Christians to be at be peace with everyone, as much as they are able to: *"Pursue peace with all men, as well as holiness, without which no one will see the Lord"* Hebrew 12:14. Let us take some time to ensure that we are wearing the shoes of peace. Please reflect and think about your relationships with others. Is there any person with whom you are not at peace? You can write your feelings below and/or take a moment to tell this to our heavenly Father, in prayer. You may refer to lesson 9, if you feel you need to confront anger and bitterness towards that particular person(s).

Christians must be ready to share the gospel of peace with humanity. The peace received by accepting the love of Jesus Christ becomes a motivation to share the good news to others, so that they too may experience the unspeakable gift. The peace from the good news enhances mental wellness and gives hope for the spiritual being, through the assurance of eternal salvation. It is not easy to explain the joy and peace brought about by the good news of Jesus Christ; the best way is to have an experience. The goodness of the experience is better described by the one who experience it. This is the reason David stated: *"Taste and see that the Lord is good. Blessed is the one who takes refuge in him."* Psalms 34:8.

Christians who share the good news are victorious: *"And they have defeated him by the blood of the Lamb and by their testimony. And they did not love their lives so much that they were afraid to die (Revelation 12:11).* The devil does not want the bride to share the good news. He justifies this act by stating that sharing the good news is a very big task which might offend the other person and that the Christian who shares the good news will be discouraged by the negative responses. While there is some truth in the above two statements, God has alerted Christians that others will reject the message of the good news. This does not mean that they reject the Christian sharing the news, but they reject Christ and He was also rejected by many when He was in this world: *"If the world hates you, keep in mind that it hated me first"* John 15:18. However, the shoes God gives us are the motivation to continue to proclaim the true peace that is only available in God through the cross of our Lord Jesus Christ. In Isaiah 52:7 and Romans 10:15 we learn that Christians who share the gospel of peace have beautiful feet. Please make notes below, on your feelings and thoughts about sharing the good news to others.

How would you like to share the good news, to who?

What are some of the challenges you might face when sharing the good news to the person named above?

What do you think is the best way to deal with the challenges named above?

When would you like to share the good news to this person(s)?

4. Shield of Faith

"Above all, taking the shield of faith with which you will be able to quench all the fiery darts of the wicked one" Ephesians 6:16

When going to the battlefield a Roman solider was to carry a large long wooden shield which was covered with strong leather. As all the pieces of the armour are a requirement in the Christian walk, so is the shield of faith, it is an essential entity, without which the Christian dies: *"the just shall live by faith"* Hebrews 10:28. To crown it all, *"without faith it is impossible to please God......"* (Hebrews 11:6).

The shield for the Roman solider was designed in such a way as to snugly fit to those of other warriors, so that an entire line of soldiers would interlock their shields to look like a solid wall and they would march to attack the enemy. This symbolises the fact that although individual Christians take the shield of faith in fighting the devil, they also live by faith as a group or collectively as the body of Christ. Hence, *'pursuing peace with all men'* as stated in Hebrews 12:4 is paramount in defeating the devil. The devil strives to remove peace and harmony among humanity; ensuring that there is division among their organisations. Examples of such organisations are: the church of the living God, families, businesses, political organisations, social gathering, to name a few. This is a doorway for the devil to rule over these organisations, thereby preventing humanity from participating in the royal wedding ceremony.

The phrase: *"above all"* is significant, because it means that in addition to all the pieces of the armour discussed above, God requires that the bride of Christ always carry the shield of faith. This phrase also implies that the shield of faith must be used under all circumstances and in all situations. Please read Hebrews 11:1, then make notes on the definition of FAITH.

Christians must use the shield of faith to protect themselves from the vicious and fiery darts, spears or arrows which come from the devil. Faith is a defensive weapon that prevents injury to the believer. During the time of Paul, the enemy intensified the impact of the spear by dipping the metal piece in an inflammable substance, so that it ignited fire when landing on their enemy. Although the darts of the devil are evident on the physical being of humanity, his (Satan) main targets are the invisible aspects of humanity: the soul and spirit. Some of the fiery darts of the devil are: lies; blasphemous thoughts, such as asserting that God does not exist; hateful thoughts about others; fear; doubt; and the urge to sin. If these darts are not quenched by faith in the life of a Christian, they ignite fire in the life of God's asset, so that humanity/Christian begin to disobey God until they become rebellious to His Word.

Fear is the opposite of faith. Fear is an emotional response in an attempt to avoid an imminent or forthcoming dangerous situation(s). Others have ascribed an acronym to define fear: **F**alse **E**vidence **A**ppearing **R**eal. The devil uses fear to paralyse humanity, so that once this spear dwells in the Christian's life they become anxious and afraid; they will not be able to fight back. Although fear is an acceptable feeling to a certain extent, prolonged or ongoing fear can have negative results to the body, such as: palpitations, heart burn, upset stomach, high blood pressure, blindness. Ongoing fear hinders productivity. However, this does not mean that those who live with the above conditions are fearful, but Satan inflicts them with false evidence which appears real.

Please take a moment and think about some of the darts which might have been sent by the enemy to you or anyone you know. Then make notes on how faith was used to protect the Christian from being injured.

Darts	Specific Situations of the Darts	How Faith is Used
Lies		
Blasphemou s thoughts		
Thoughts of hate		
Doubt		
Urge to sin		
Bad thoughts		
Illness		
Regret		
Failure		
Fear		
Death		

The devil does not have a specified time and day to attack the children of God, in fact he is always roaming around like a lion, looking for people to devour (1 Peter 5:8). This means then that the whole armour must be in place, at all times. Having the shield of faith correctly placed (covering the whole body at the front) provides the Christian with dynamic power to bravely stand against the devil. The shield forms a very strong wall in front of the bride, so that the devil is unable to reach the army of God.

The use of the shield of faith allows believers to have a testimony, they are able to share the good news of God's provision and intervention during challenging times: *"For by it (faith) the elders obtained a good testimony"* Hebrews 11:2.

5. *Helmet of salvation*

"Put on salvation as your helmet......" Ephesians 6:17

During the first century the Roman soldiers wore a metal helmet to protect them against the blows of the enemy to their head. We shall remember from previous lessons that salvation means that humanity is saved from eternal death by choosing to accept the love of Jesus Christ and allow Him to reign in their lives. It is important for humanity to be saved from sin (John 3:3-7) and this is the first step in the Christian journey or the step in reconciling humanity with their creator.

All Christians must put on the helmet of salvation, which means that their minds and thinking must **be controlled by God and the Holy Spirit**. Salvation brings about the renewal of the mind. *"I appeal to you therefore, brothers, by the mercies of God, to present your bodies as a living sacrifice, holy and acceptable to God, which is your spiritual worship. Do not be conformed to this world, but be transformed by the renewal of your mind, that by testing you may discern what is the will of God, what is good and acceptable and perfect.* Romans 12:1-2. Kindly make notes on what the above verse means to you.

The renewed mind plays a significant role to Christians in their spiritual growth, victory and service unto the Lord. Allowing God to take control of the mind is a powerful weapon to fight the devil, because such Christians have hope at all times. Hope for daily living and eternal salvation. Even when going through difficult situations a Christians who has put on the helmet of salvation are sustained and they overcome, because of the hope and anchor in the Lord our God. The transition from worldly thinking to being Godly in the mind can be tricky and difficult. Please read Philippians 4:8. This verse enumerates what Christians must always think about.

Even though they endeavour to always think about good things at all times, as stated in Philippians, Christians are not immune to experiencing suffering. Please read the following verses and make notes on the suffering of the children of God.

2 Corinthians 4:8-10

Romans 5: 3-5

The renewed state of mind is important, because it takes away all the fears brought to a Christian by the devil. The helmet of salvation enhances a stable mind, as stated: *"For God hath not given us the spirit of fear, but of power, and of love and of sound mind"* 2 Timothy 1:7.

God commands all Christians to think like Christ. *"In your lives you must think and act like Christ. Christ himself was like God in everything. But he did not think that being equal with God was something to be used for his own benefit. But He gave up His place with God and made himself nothing. He was born to be a man and became like a servant. And when he was living as a man, he humbled himself and was fully obedient to God, even when that caused his death—death on the cross."* Philippians 2:5-8. Please read the previous verse then state how else the bride of Christ must think.

When he wrote to the Philippians, Paul urged the church to fill their minds with good thoughts, as he stated in Philippians 4:8. Christians fill their minds with good thoughts by dwelling and being engrossed in the Word of God. The Word of God is Jesus Christ, He teaches Christian how to fight and conquer the devil, just as Jesus conquered the world. Please read the verses in Ephesians 4:21-24.

6. The Sword of the Spirit

"......and take the sword of the Spirit, which is the Word of God"
Ephesians 6:17

The sword of the Spirit represents the Word of God. It is a very powerful weapon, which is sharper than a double-edged sword Hebrews 4:12. This piece of armour is a requirement for the victory of the bride against their enemy. The Word of God is offensive to the devil. The power of the Word of God is revealed when humanity repent from their sin to accept the love of Jesus Christ. While the visible sword cause injury to the physical body, the Word of God pierces the heart, convicts people of their sins and enlighten them about the immeasurable love of God (Acts 2:37; 1 Peter 1:23). The Word of God also provides nutrients to the soul and spirit, because it reaches to the inner being of humanity. Please read the following verses and make comments on how the Word of God feeds the invisible being.

Joshua 1:8

Jeremiah 15:16

Matthew 4:4

John 6:49-51

The visible sword gets worn out and becomes blunt with repeated usage, but the opposite is true about the sword of the Spirit/ the Word of God; it becomes sharper in the lives of those who use it. While the visible sword cannot function without being in the hand of the warrior, the sword of the Spirit has its unique power and ability to function independently, even without restrictions of boundaries. When used the physical sword causes injury and appearance of wounds or damage to the body; yet the sword of the Spirit causes wounds to heal and it gives life. To crown it ALL, when used against the devil the sword of the Spirit knocks him down, paralyses him and stops him from hindering the smooth running of the work of God. According to 2 Corinthians 10: 3-5 this weapon is powerful and mighty to pull down strongholds of the devil, destroy obstacles and capture rebellious thoughts.

Satan knows the Word of God very well; he uses the same Word to lie and try to confuse humanity. Even though the devil actually quotes the Word of God as it is written, his quotes are out of context; he also leaves out other words so that the quote suits or justifies his point of argument. When tempted by the devil Jesus stated that *"it is written......"* Luke 4:1-13, yet because the devil also imitates God, he also stated *"it is written......"* Luke 4:10.

During a recent conversation between my eldest son and a family friend, my son stated that God does not love him, because of the verse in Genesis 6:6 *"And the Lord was sorry that He had made man on the earth......"* The irony of this lie from the devil is that God used the same verse to open my heart to accept His love; I repented when the same verse was preached on 25/03/1982. For this reason, Christians must carry the sword of the spirit at all times; they must read and know the Word of God, so that they are able to use it to attack the devil when he tries to wrongly quote the word of God.

Please take a moment and reflect on your experience, regarding how the devil lies or has lied about the Word of God. Make a note of the lies from the devil, stating how they are quoted out of context and then state the meaning of the text from God's perspective.

OVERCOMING THROUGH PRAYER

"praying always with all prayer and supplication in the Spirit, at all times and on every occasion. Stay alert and be persistent in your prayers for all believers everywhere. And pray for me too. Ask God to give me the right words so I can boldly explain God's mysterious plan that the Good News is for Jew and Gentiles alike." Ephesians 6:18-19.

Prayer can also be defined as a friendly progressive interaction between the living God and humanity. This is a continuous and non-formal communion of humanity with their creator, with the knowledge and confidence about the unconditional love of their creator. During this time an individual sends messages of petition and/or thanksgiving to God. Importantly to note is the fact that humanity gets an opportunity to listen and hear from God. Prayer is the act of changing a situation for the better. After they learnt that Haman had planned to kill the Jews; with the influence from Mordechai, Esther and the rest of the Jews engaged in prayer and God changed the situation. Instead of hanging Mordechai, Haman was hung on the same gallows he had prepared to hang Mordecai.

"Prayer is the energy that enables the Christian soldier to wear the armour and wield the sword. We cannot fight the battle in our own power, no matter how strong or talented we may think we are." (Wiersbe, Warren W. The Wiersbe Commentary, pg642). To answer the question on how a Christian should pray in order to defeat Satan, Paul delineated six ways in which the Christian should pray: **always pray; pray with all prayer; pray in the Spirit; pray with your eyes open; pray continuously and pray for all saints.**

- *Always pray*

Praying at all times means that Christians must always be in communion or fellowship with God; praying without ceasing as stated in 1 Thessalonians 5:17. This is one of the ways to ensure that Satan is defeated when he attack them with his darts, spears and temptations. One might wonder what it is that Christians should say or commune to God about. This is an important question, which was also asked by the disciples of Jesus, saying *"Teach us how to pray"* Luke 11:1. Jesus informed his disciples that they should not say empty words during prayer, because a lot of empty words do not have meaning before God (Matthew 6:7). We are ever so grateful to the Holy Spirit who is able to teach us how to pray and also take our petitions and intercessions to our Heavenly Father (Romans 8:26-27).

- *Pray with all prayer*

Before I learnt more about prayer, I thought that prayer only consisted of asking God to do things for me so that His power would be revealed. I have since learnt that there are different types of prayers with which Christians defeat the enemy. Paul instructed the bride of Christ to pray all types of prayer. As already discussed in previous lessons, Christians are humans who have confessed and forsaken their sins and have been forgiven by God, because of His grace revealed through the Lord Jesus Christ. However, while they walk and live around the world, Christians are tempted and they can find themselves committing sin: knowingly or unknowingly (Psalms 19:12). This means that the prayer of **confession** of sin is an ongoing, progressive prayer for the bride of Christ. It is one way of living a righteous life and allows the bride to keep their wedding garment spotless, by regularly immersing their garment in the blood of the Lamb (Revelation 22:14). This does not mean that Christians should sin deliberately, with the knowledge that they will ask for forgiveness, because this leads to God's judgement: *"For if we sin wilfully after we have received the knowledge of the truth, there no longer remains a sacrifice for sins, but a certain fearful expectation of judgement, and fiery indignation which will devour the adversaries"* Hebrews 10:26-27.

If we harbour sin in the heart, God does not hear our prayers: *"If I regard or harbour iniquity in my heart, the Lord will not hear me"* Psalms 66:18. This situation provides a doorway for the devil to influence the believer to doubt the power and love of God, so that their faith in God becomes eroded. This type of Christian puts away their shield of faith, thereby becoming exposed to the shots, arrows and darts of the devil. The good news is that if we confession our sins; that is owning up to sin and asking for God's mercy and forgiveness, He is faithful, just and willing to forgive us all our sins, always (1 John 1:9).

Additionally, hiding sin from God does not only affect the spiritual being of humanity, but also has negative impact to the physical being. David stated: *"When I kept silent about my sin, my body wasted away through my groaning all day long. For day and night Your hand was heavy upon me; my vitality was drained away as with the fever heat of summer......I acknowledged my sin to You, and my iniquity I did not hide; I said, "I will confess my sin to the Lord"; and You forgave the guilt of my sin"* (Psalms 32:4-5). Unconfessed sin affects the emotional, spiritual and physical being of humanity, the only relief is found through confessing and leaving the sinful habit. Please spend a brief quiet moment and reflect on your life, with the help of the Holy

Spirit identify any sin in your life which could hinder your prayers. Take some time to confess any identified sin and those which might have been knowingly or unknowingly committed. Make notes on these and how you feel after the prayer.

David said: *"Enter his gates with **thanksgiving**; go into his courts with praise. Give thanks to him and praise His name"* Psalms 100:4. In Philippians 4:6-7 Paul affirms that thanking God is an emotional therapeutic tool which alleviates distress; and therefore, promotes the mental wellbeing for those who thank God at all times, even during difficult times. Please take a moment to think about what God has done for you, make a list below then take some time to thank Him for these things.

The third strategy to defeat the devil is by ***praising and adoring*** God. This is where the Christian shows respect, reverence, strong admiration and devotion to the one and only living God. This type of prayer provides Christians with the opportunity to praise God for His greatness, grace and faithfulness. They also admit their full dependence on Him. This act does not give the devil chance to dwell in the lives of the Christian, because God dwells in the praises of His people, as stated: *"But thou art holy, O thou that inhabitest the praises of Israel"* Psalms 22: 3.

The power of praise and worshipping God was clearly evident when Paul and Silas were chained in prison. Instead of mourning and complaining they did not only pray, but started worshipping the Lord at midnight. The presence of the Lord made the foundation of the prison to be shaken, the doors were opened, chains of all the prisoners were loosen and more people were added into the kingdom of God, because the prison keeper and his family accepted Jesus Christ as their Lord and Saviour Acts: 16:25-34.

The plans and works of the devil are demolished when Christians engage in ***prayer of supplication or intercession***. The word 'supplication' means a request or petition. This is the prayer whereby Christians ask God for something; either for themselves, others or both. It is important for the bride to send their supplications and petitions to God, according to His will and not theirs. As such, the motive of a praying Christian must be that the answers to the petition would give glory and honour to the Lord *"And this is the confidence that we have toward Him, that if we ask anything according to His will he hears us. And if we know that He hears us in whatever we ask, we know that we have the requests that we have asked of him"* (1 John 5:14-15). Paul informed the church that we are not fighting against flesh and blood, but against principalities, against the rulers of the darkness of his age and against powers in heavenly places (Ephesians 6:12-13). The prayer of intercession scatters and demolishes the works of the devil in the spiritual realm, as stated in 2 Corinthians 10: 3-5. Please read and reflect on the scripture in Ezekiel 22:30. Take a moment of silence and make notes on what you would like to do about *'standing in the gap'*.

- *Pray in the Spirit*

Christians are to pray to God the Father through Jesus Christ His son and in the Spirit, at all times. Praying with divine help from the Holy Spirit. Praying in the Spirit allows God's children to pray according to His will, as opposed to praying according to their selfish motives. The Holy Spirit has a very significant role in humanity, because He intercedes for humanity with groaning which cannot be uttered, Romans 8:26-27. When a Christian prays in the Spirit it means that they completely trust and rely on God for help; and are confident that He hears and understands their prayers and that He will/is acting accordingly.

- *Pray with your eyes open*

When he was about to be crucified Jesus went up to pray on the mountain of Gethsemane, with His disciples. He was becoming sorrowful and deeply distressed. Although He had asked His disciples to pray with Him, they were overcome by sleep. Jesus warned His disciples saying: *"Watch and pray, lest you enter into temptation......"* Matthew 26:41. In the previous lesson we saw that Jesus emphasised the importance of being alert or being watchful as we wait for His return to take His bride to heaven.

Nehemiah sets an example of how Christians should pray with their eyes opened. While pursuing their God given task (rebuilding the walls of Jerusalem) Nehemiah was faced with opponents, wanting to stop him from completing the project. They defeated their enemies by praying with their eyes opened: *"Nevertheless we made our prayer unto our God, and set a watch"* (Nehemiah 4:9). Through prayer the Holy Spirit always guides the children of God and open their spiritual eyes, so that they are able to discern and detect the attacks of the devil.

- *Pray continuously*

God delights in ongoing fellowship and communion with humanity. We will remember that after He had created humanity in the Garden of Eden He visited them every sunset. As such, we are commissioned to always pray, at all times: *"Pray without ceasing"* 1 Thessalonians 5:17. This is a way of communing and/or being in fellowship with God.

Christians must persevere in prayer, meaning that they must keep praying and never stop.

Jesus told His disciples a parable of the persistent widow Luke 18:1-8; teaching them that Christians must pray continuously and not stop, until the Holy Spirit says otherwise. I remember praying for my two younger sisters when they were teenagers. They had not accepted Jesus as their Lord and Saviour. I was led to fast for then, but on the fifth day of prayer and fasting the Holy Spirit told me to stop asking for their repentance, but to thank Him and wait for the manifestation of my request. A year later they both accepted Jesus Christ as their Lord and Saviour. Indeed, God answers prayers, we are to pray continuously, with the help of the Holy Spirit. Please read the verses in Luke 18:1-8 then make notes on the lessons you get from the story.

- *Pray for all saints*

Christians are the body of Christ. The human physical body is one unit (system, whole) with different and many parts (subsystems) large, medium and small. Some parts are visible and others are enclosed. All body parts are essential for the proper functioning of the whole body and sustaining the life of the whole body. A disturbance to one part adversely affects the whole body, reducing optimum functioning. In a similar way, Christians all over the world are different, they have different gifts and talents, all are necessary for the proper functioning of the 'whole' body of Christ. When one Christian suffers, other Christians experience the negative effects.

During his prayer Jesus petitioned His father to unite the church, just like He and God are one (John 17:21). For this reason, Christians must pray for each other, because the victory of one brings victory to all

Christians. Praying for all saints defeats the devil by promoting peace and harmony with every believer, because by praying for each other Christians show their love for one another. The peace among the saints is a powerful channel for the presence of the Lord (Psalms 133:1-3), which means that the devil has no room among the body of Christ. Additionally, the unity in the body of Christ brings blessings to the whole body of Christ.

Please read the text in 1 Corinthians 12:12-31 and make notes on how the devil is defeated when saints pray for one another.

All in all, we realise that Christians who want to live a victorious life must put on the whole armour of God, otherwise the devil steals, kills and destroys them before they arrive at the royal wedding feast. The followers of Christ were called Christians (one who follows Christ) for the first time in Antioch (Acts 11:26). This is very important, because those who gave them this name realised that they behaved like Jesus Christ. Being Christ-like is revealed through wearing the whole armour of God, because we confirm that we are wearing Christ, as stated by Paul in Romans 13:4 *"Instead, clothe yourself with the presence of the Lord Jesus Christ. And don't let yourself think about ways to indulge your evil desires"*.

Please take some time to look at the table below and read the verses which describe the Lord Jesus, in relation to the armour of God. Then complete the last column, allocating the description of Jesus in relation to the armour.

JESUS CHRIST IS

HE IS	THE WORD	THE ARMOUR
Truth	John 14:6	
Righteousness	2 Corinthians 5:21	
Our peace	Ephesians 2:14	
Faithful and fuels our faith	Galatians 2:20	
Our salvation	Luke 2:30	
The Word of God	John 1:1, 14	

Are you Insured?

Choosing to accept Jesus Christ as your Lord and Saviour and living a life set apart for God is the true insurance of the soul and spirit of humanity. Let us take some time to think about insurance. Please complete the following questions:

What do you understand is the meaning of the word 'insurance'?

Please name some of the insurance companies you know, or those you find on Google?

Make a list of the things that are insured by the various insurance companies.

Think about your experience or any information you have about how one benefited from the insurance company to which they are members, when they needed to claim. Make notes on how they benefited from the insurance company and the disadvantages they could have incurred if they were not insured during the time of the accident/incident which led to their claim.

Please note that all the above is very important and useful in insuring physical things. Accepting Jesus Christ as your Lord and Saviour and living a life set apart for God is assurance of eternal life and everlasting fellowship with our God. Therefore, seeing that humanity is a whole, divided into three aspects; it is wisdom to be insured in ALL the three aspects. If we have life insurance, car insurance, house insurance, then it is the best choice to accept the free insurance of the spirit. Please, please, please, be assured that your spirit is insured, because it is eternal.

Please note that in the last days, some people will think that God and His Word are not important. People will turn away from God; they will believe that the Word of God is not true, and that it is stupid and silly 2 Timothy 3:1-9. As a result, they ridicule Christians; calling them fools because of their belief in the living God. These people will do whatever bad things they want to do. They will believe that Christ will not return to earth again, because "He promised this a long time ago and has not even returned, up to this time". They also argue that the early Christians also said the same thing that Christ would return to earth, but He has not done it up to now. However, God is very patient with humanity, wishing that NOBODY perishes in hell, God is patient so that, perhaps more and more people would accept His love and invitation to the royal wedding feast *"The Lord is not slack concerning his promise, as some men count slackness; but is longsuffering to us-*

ward, not willing that any should perish, but that ALL should come to repentance" 2 Peter 3:9.

Some people choose to forget the facts and/or perhaps belittle or undermine the Word of God. They think they are in charge and in control, but no, God is in control of this world and everything in it. He does things as He desires. It does not mean that because He is quiet and looking at all the evil going on in the earth that He is incapable to intervene, He only makes all things beautiful, in His time. God spoke His Word, and so he made the sky. Also, by His Word, God made the land separate from the water. He brought the land out through the water (2 Peter 3:5). God is in control. Those who choose to deny this will soon see, because every knee will soon bow and every tongue will confess that Jesus Christ is Lord. Hallelujah! Amen!

> *'For the scriptures say, "As surely as I live," says the LORD, "every knee will bow to me, and every tongue will declare allegiance to God."* **Romans 14:11**

So, why wait, it's better we start now to worship and confess that the one and only God is Lord, because one day, very soon EVERYONE must worship God, whether they like it or not.

SUMMARY

Humanity was created by God in His image. God put His breath in the nostrils of humanity and they became living beings. Their roles are: to be fruitful, multiply, dominate and be stewards of the earth and everything in it. God gave humanity the power of the 'will'; the ability to make choices on everything or anything they desire. God then commanded them to subdue the earth. God intended to maintain an eternal relationship with humanity. Lucifer once lived in heaven as the head angel of worship. He became proud, sinned by wanting to be like God and was chased out of heaven; his eternal destination is hell, where he will be tortured and tormented forever, along with all who choose to follow him.

The relationship between humanity and God was interrupted by sin, Adam and Eve disobeyed God, by accepting the information from the devil; to eat of the forbidden fruit at the centre of the garden. Their spiritual lineage was changed because of the seed of evil which was planted by the devil. However, because of His everlasting love, grace, mercy and kindness God sent His only son to die for humanity (at the cross of Calvary). Jesus came to redeem humanity. Those who choose to accept the love of God are referred to as Christians, because they are born again. They are also known as the bride of Christ. One day very soon Jesus will return to the earth for His bride and will take her to heaven where there will be a wedding celebration for her and Jesus, her bridegroom. Jesus is presently preparing mansions for His bride. As a result, humanity does not need to die, but can receive eternal life by accepting the love of Jesus Christ into their lives. Their names are written in The Book of Life and they receive a special garment; a prerequisite for entering the royal wedding feast.

The devil does not want humanity to have a relationship with God, their creator. He lived in heaven and knows that it is a beautiful place. Nothing on earth can compare and even properly describe the heavenly beauty. The goal of Satan is to steal, kill and destroy and his target is God's asset: humanity. As such, he is constantly fighting humanity every moment of their lives: he blinds them so that they decline God's love until they die and join him in hell; where there is eternal separation from God. For those who accept Jesus as their Lord and Saviour the devil fights them, in an attempt to draw them back to sin (backslide). This means that while they are in this world humanity is constantly at war with the devil. The good news is that humanity was designed to overcome the devil and they overcome, not through their own strength, but through the power of the Holy Spirit and through Jesus Christ our Lord, who lives in them and in whom they are hidden, in heavenly places. Hallelujah! Amen! The whole armour of God is humanity's spiritual attire used to conquer all the tactics of the devil. At the end of the present life God will gather the world so that each and every person will give an account of their lives on this earth and they will receive rewards according to what they have done while living on this world.

As you continue this life's warfare, I would recommend that you proceed to read *"The Armor of God"* by Priscilla Shirer. This book will help you to fight a good fight of faith as you get ready to enter the royal wedding feast.

You are sincerely loved blessed and highly favoured by God the Father, God the Son and God the Holy Spirit. I really look forward to the greatest soon coming family reunion, I will be looking out for you and I pray you will do the same for all the people of God, including me. Halleluiah! Amen!

REFLECTIVE NOTES & PRAYER
LESSON 1

It is wonderful that you have completed all the lessons within this book. Please spend some time to reflect on each of the lessons. Below are blank pages for you to make notes on things which are outstanding for you. You will realise that the Holy Spirit will reveal to you a lot of things which you can make notes on the spaces below. Please also write your prayers in the spaces provided as you make notes on your reflection. You are God's treasure and asset, remain blessed now and always.

REFLECTIVE NOTES & PRAYER
LESSON 2

REFLECTIVE NOTES & PRAYER
LESSON 3

REFLECTIVE NOTES & PRAYER
LESSON 4

REFLECTIVE NOTES & PRAYER
LESSON 5

REFLECTIVE NOTES & PRAYER
LESSON 6

REFLECTIVE NOTES & PRAYER
LESSON 7

REFLECTIVE NOTES & PRAYER
LESSON 8

REFLECTIVE NOTES & PRAYER
LESSON 9

REFLECTIVE NOTES & PRAYER
LESSON 10

REFLECTIVE NOTES & PRAYER
LESSON 11

BIBLIOGRAPHY

Aptowitzert V. Asenath, *The Wife Of Joseph: A Haggadic Literary-Historical Study*. New York: Hebrew Union College Press, 1924, Vol. 1 pp. 239-306.

Blomberg Craig L, *Jesus and the Gospels: New Testament Introduction and Survey* (2nd Ed.) Nottingham: Inter-Varsity Press, 2009.

Bruce FF. *The International Bible Commentary With the New International Version*. Michigan: Zondervan Publishing House, 1986.

Carson, D.A, France, R. T., Motyer, J. A., Wenham, G. J. (Editors). *New Bible Commentary*. Nottingham: Intervarsity Press, 2011.

Christin Gerard A. *The bible panorama: enjoying the whole bible with a chapter by chapter guide 3rd Ed.* Leominster: One day publications, 2015.

Church, Lesley F. (Editor). *Matthew Henry's Commentary In one volume*. Michigan: Zondervan, 1962.

Fiorenza, Elisabeth Schussler. *Searching the Scriptures A Feminist Commentary Vol. 2*. London: SCM Press LTD, 1995.

Hindson, Edward E. and Mitchell, Daniel R. (Ed.) *King James Version Commentary*. (Michigan: Zondervan), 2011.

House, Paul R. *Isaiah A mentor Commentary*. Glasgow: Christian Focus Publication, 2019.

https://study.com/academy/lesson/omnipotent-omniscient-and-omnipresent-god-definition-lesson-quiz.html

Hunt John (Ed.). *"What does every Bible chapter say…." The Ultimate Bible Outline/Theme book*. (Tennesse: John Hunt Publishing Ltd), 2011.

Longman III, Tremper & Garland David E. (Ed.) *The Expositor's Bible Commentary Proverbs-Isaiah*. (Michigan: Zondervan).

Longenecker, Richard N. *The New International Greek Testament Commentary: The Epistle of the Romans*. (Michigan: William B. Eerdmans Publishing Company), 2016

Motyer Alec. *The Bible speaks today: Message of Job*. Nottingham: InterVarsity Press

Noble T.A. *Holy Trinity: Holy People The Theology of Christian Perfecting*. Cambridge: James Clarke and Company, 2013.

Nxumalo-Ngubane. *The Experiences, Perceptions and Meaning of Recovery for Swazi women living with Sifo Sengcondvo 'Schizophrenia'* University of Salford, UK School of Nursing, Midwifery Social Work & Social Science: Thesis Submitted in Partial fulfilment for the requirements of the degree of Doctor of Philosophy November 2016

Powell Mark Allan. *Introducing The New Testament: A Historical, Literary, And Theological Survey* 2nd Ed. Michigan: Baker Academic.

Shirer Pricilla. *The Armor of God*. Nashville: Adult Ministry Publishing, 2019.

Smith William, *Smith's Bible Dictionary*. Massachusetts: Hendrickson Publishers Marketing, LLC), 2014.

Walvoord John F. and Zuck Roy B. (Ed). *The Bible Knowledge Commentary Wisdom*. Sussex: David C Cook, 2018.

Wiersbe, Warren W. *The Wiersbe Commentary: the complete Old Testament in one volume*. Sussex: David C Cook, 2007.

Wiersbe, Warren W. *The Wiersbe Commentary: the complete New Testament in one volume*. Sussex: David C Cook, 2007.

http://markgoodacre.org/aseneth/translat.htm *Joseph & Aseneth: Translated by David Cook*. Hyptertext version by Dr Mark Goodacre, University of Birmingham

https://en.wikipedia.org/wiki/Diana_Princes of Wale

A Commissioned Publication Printed by

MOORLEYS
Print, Design & Publishing
info@moorleys.co.uk • www.moorleys.co.uk